Jammie Price

Navigating Differences
Friendships Between
Gay and Straight Men

Pre-publication
REVIEW

"*N*avigating Differences provides a thoughtful and thought-provoking look at the rare world of friendships between gay and straight men. By presenting these friendships not as accomplished facts but as ongoing processes, Price offers us a sensitive description of the struggles of these men to grow individually and together. As she shows us, these friendships, while often difficult, hold both a promise of great personal satisfaction for those men who master their challenges and avenues to dismantle heterosexism and hegemonic masculinity.

Price's account is equally important for her approach to research. She is no dispassionate researcher. Rather her commitment to her participants and active involvement in their struggles for social justice provide an invaluable model for all academics who care for those they study. Her efforts—both her good work in this book and her 'good works' in her community—enrich all of us who care about sexual and gender equality."

Shealy Thompson, PhD
Researcher, Center for Urban Affairs and Community Service,
North Carolina State University

Navigating Differences
Friendships Between Gay and Straight Men

HAWORTH Gay & Lesbian Studies
John P. De Cecco, PhD
Editor in Chief

New, Recent, and Forthcoming Titles:

Gay and Lesbian Mental Health: A Sourcebook for Practitioners edited by Christopher J. Alexander

Against My Better Judgment: An Intimate Memoir of an Eminent Gay Psychologist by Roger Brown

The Masculine Marine: Homoeroticism in the U.S. Marine Corps by Steven Zeeland

Bisexual Characters in Film: From Anaïs to Zee by Wayne M. Bryant

The Bear Book: Readings in the History and Evolution of a Gay Male Subculture edited by Les Wright

Youths Living with HIV: Self-Evident Truths by G. Cajetan Luna

Growth and Intimacy for Gay Men: A Workbook by Christopher J. Alexander

Our Families, Our Values: Snapshots of Queer Kinship edited by Robert E. Goss and Amy Adams Squire Strongheart

Gay/Lesbian/Bisexual/Transgender Public Policy Issues: A Citizen's and Administrator's Guide to the New Cultural Struggle edited by Wallace Swan

Rough News, Daring Views: 1950s' Pioneer Gay Press Journalism by Jim Kepner

Family Secrets: Gay Sons—A Mother's Story by Jean M. Baker

Twenty Million New Customers: Understanding Gay Men's Consumer Behavior by Steven M. Kates

The Empress Is a Man: Stories from the Life of José Sarria by Michael R. Gorman

Acts of Disclosure: The Coming-Out Process of Contemporary Gay Men by Marc E. Vargo

Queer Kids: The Challenges and Promise for Lesbian, Gay, and Bisexual Youth by Robert E. Owens

Looking Queer: Body Image and Identity in Lesbian, Gay, Bisexual, and Transgender Communities edited by Dawn Atkins

Love and Anger: Essays on AIDS, Activism, and Politics by Peter F. Cohen

Dry Bones Breathe: Gay Men Creating Post-AIDS Identities and Cultures by Eric Rofes

Lila's House: Male Prostitution in Latin America by Jacobo Schifter

A Consumer's Guide to Male Hustlers by Joseph Itiel

Trailblazers: Profiles of America's Gay and Lesbian Elected Officials by Kenneth E. Yeager

Rarely Pure and Never Simple: Selected Essays of Scott O'Hara by Scott O'Hara

Navigating Differences: Friendships Between Gay and Straight Men by Jammie Price

In the Pink: The Making of Successful Gay- and Lesbian-Owned Businesses by Sue Levin

Behold the Man: The Hype and Selling of Male Beauty in Media and Culture by Edisol Wayne Dotson

Untold Millions: The Truth About Marketing to Gay and Lesbian Consumers by Grant Lukenbill

It's a Queer World: Deviant Adventures in Pop Culture by Mark Simpson

In Your Face: Stories from the Lives of Queer Youth by Mary L. Gray

Navigating Differences
Friendships Between
Gay and Straight Men

Jammie Price

Harrington Park Press
An Imprint of The Haworth Press, Inc.
New York • London

Published by

Harrington Park Press, an imprint of The Haworth Press, Inc., 10 Alice Street, Binghamton, NY 13904-1580

Cover design by Marylouise E. Doyle.

The Library of Congress has cataloged the hardcover edition of this book as:

Price, Jammie.
   Navigating differences : friendships between gay and straight men / Jammie Price.
     p. cm.
   Includes bibliographical references and index.
   ISBN 0-7890-0619-7 (alk. paper)
    1. Male friendship. 2. Men—Psychology. 3. Gay men—Psychology. I. Title.
BF692.P75 1999
302.3′4′081—dc21   98-28103
                                                            CIP

ISBN 1-56023-952-2 (pbk.)

I dedicate this book to my mother, Terrie O'Brien, and to my husband's father, Claiborne Whitehead. While I was conducting this research, my mother faced astounding life challenges. Her struggles constantly reminded me of the real world, of concerns and needs much more significant than those of the academic world of ideas and words. Similarly, Claiborne Whitehead constantly reminded me of what is truly important in life. His integrity, devotion, responsibility, and generosity define for me what a man can and should be. Although I never had the privilege of meeting him, his influence on my husband blesses my life every day.

ABOUT THE AUTHOR

Jammie Price, PhD, is a Research Coordinator for University Health Systems and an Adjunct Assistant Sociology Professor at East Carolina University in Greenville, North Carolina. Her professional interests center on gender, social psychology, and research methods and analysis. Dr. Price's substantive interests focus on how men reproduce gender and sexual inequalities through their everyday interaction with other men. A specialist in action research, Dr. Price, a married, straight woman, cofounded a local grassroots organization devoted to establishing sexual equality. She has held an executive office in this organization, including President and Chair of the Board of Directors, for the past four years.

CONTENTS

Foreword

Dr. Jammie Price's study of men's friendships is a thorough, well-written exploration of identity, gender, sexuality, and emotions in uncommon friendships between gay and straight men. She has conducted probing and insightful interviews with more than twenty-five pairs of close friends. The interviews cover topics ranging from how the gay men came out to their straight friends, to how straight men deal with their gay friends' HIV status and AIDS. The interviews are poignant and bring the reader into the emotional lives of these friends.

Dr. Price explores how the men's individual identities grow and change as they negotiate their differences to create strong friendships. She provides an intimate account of these men's personal and public struggles with homophobia. But the research is optimistic because her findings clearly indicate that straight and gay men can move beyond homophobia and at least accept their differences, if not respect them.

This work is important on several fronts. First, we can learn much about theoretical issues relating to gender from a study of men negotiating new ways to interact without clear dependence on hegemonic notions of masculinity. Second, the author skillfully explores the emotional strategies used in shaping the relationship between gender and sexuality, adding to our general knowledge of emotion work. Finally, Dr. Price takes the reader to the logical conclusion of this research and shows what kinds of future efforts are needed to reduce homophobia and inequality between and among men.

The writing is powerful and straightforward. The book is sure to be appealing to students and general readers as well as academic researchers. Sociologists, psychologists, therapists, and gay men and those who live with them and love them will all want to read this book.

Barbara Risman, PhD
Department of Sociology
North Carolina State University
Raleigh, NC

Preface

My sociological interests have always centered around inequality—namely, how do we get people to stop treating each other inequitably? How do we get people to treat one another with respect? Or, more specifically, how do we get people to follow the golden rule—to treat others as you would have them treat you? When I was planning this study, the inequality that most disturbed me was heterosexism and homophobia. As Herek (1984a) explained, homophobia refers to a fear of or discomfort with nonheterosexual people; while heterosexism refers to beliefs and values which posit that nonheterosexual people are inferior to heterosexual people and to the behaviors which create or reproduce heterosexual privilege.

All around me I saw people, both straight and gay, both feminist and nonfeminist, act heterosexist or homophobic, in public and in private. It was subtle at times, blatant at others. While I was finishing this study, some four years later, our social climate began changing. Gay issues were getting attention in mainstream newspapers and magazines, and within a year or two, it seemed every prime time television show had at least one gay character. Suddenly, we are surrounded by gay issues, at times subtle, and at times blatant. Although the change is refreshing, I still worry about the central issue—are we treating each other with respect? For the most part, I think the answer remains "no."

I began planning the study by looking for examples of gay and straight people who did treat each with respect. I decided to focus on friendships between gay and straight men for two reasons. One, I chose to focus on men exclusively because I think in the United States, people, particularly straight men, are more homophobic and heterosexist with gay men than with lesbians. Lesbians do not seem to threaten our beliefs, our values, our lives as much as gay men. And, two, I chose to focus on friendships because they are informal, voluntary interactions. They are not bounded by rules or regulations, and as such, offer a clearer window into social behavior.

My goal for this study was to understand friendships between gay and straight men. I wanted to know the men and their lives and what enabled them to be friends. I wanted to know what they did in their friendships, how the friendships began and evolved. I wanted to know the value of the friendship to these men and the role it played in their lives. From this I hoped to understand how to motivate other people to act similarly—how to put aside differences, stereotypes, and prejudices, and treat each other with respect.

This book unfolds as follows. In the Introduction, I explain how and why the study came about. In Chapter 1, I review the literature on men's friendships, emotion, gender, and sexuality. In Chapter 2, I describe my research methods, including my data collection, analysis, and sample characteristics. Also, I introduce the reader to the three types of friendships: friends who embrace their sexual differences, friends who ignore their differences, and friends who are struggling with their differences. In Chapters 3, 4, and 5, I describe each of these types of friends, focusing on how they spend time together, express and manage emotion, and deal with their sexual differences.

In Chapter 6, I draw on the sociology of gender and sexuality to explain why some of the friends are more accepting and respecting of their sexual differences, and subsequently why some friends are closer, more emotionally intimate, and more trusting than others. I argue that the friends in each group sustain, resist, and oppose hegemonic masculinity. In Chapter 7, I offer some methodological reflections on this project, identifying the potential biases and limitations of my study and the impact of the study on the lives of the men I interviewed. Finally in Chapter 8, I review my role as a participatory researcher. Here I discuss how my participation in a community action organization influenced this research and how my sociological expertise influenced my role in the organization.

Jammie Price

Acknowledgments

I am grateful to many people for their help with this project. First and foremost, I am greatly appreciative of the men who shared their lives and friendships with me. Second, I want to thank Barbara Risman for her constructive criticism and guidance. Thanks to Kristen Myers, Cathy Zimmer, and Ron Czaja for their advice and encouragement. I thank the Levine Memorial Dissertation Fellowship for helping to fund this research. Finally, I am deeply grateful to my husband, John Whitehead, for his limitless support.

Introduction

As a feminist, I care deeply about justice between men and women, as well as between different kinds of men. Most sociological research and theory on gender inequality has focused on relations between men and women. This misses the area in which a great deal of gender inequality originates—interactions between men. In a world where men principally hold and determine power and privilege, men's greatest threat for these privileges and power comes from similarly entitled individuals—other men, not women (Segal, 1990; Reskin, 1988). Consequently, men worry most about their positions relative to other men. The motivation to be masculine, or to "do gender" (West and Zimmerman, 1987), becomes heightened when men are with men (Morgan, 1992; Messner, 1992). And, by doing this among themselves, men contribute to the reproduction of gender inequality.

So I ask, how do we get men to stop reproducing gender inequality? The sociology of masculinity arose to answer this very question. Research in this field has tried to explain how and why men do gender. If we can understand what, how, and why, maybe we can encourage men to change. We have learned a great deal from the research in this field, but most men have not changed significantly. Some men do resist and oppose gendered power and privileges with women, but not many. The culturally ideal or, as Connell (1987) coined, "hegemonic" way that men signify being men in the United States today is still to display an ability to compete relative to other men, reject effeminacy, and express heterosexual desire.

I decided it was time to take a different strategy in studying gender among men. I wanted to look at men who do not act hegemonically with other men and determine why they do not. This exploration, I thought, might reveal how to motivate other men to act similarly. The next step was to pick a group of men to study. I could have studied men in feminist movements or in friendships between white and black men. I chose to study friendships between gay and straight men. I did so for the following reasons.

Friendships between gay and straight men are rare (Nardi, 1992a,b). A wealth of research is available to draw on to understand why. Research has well established that men's attitudes toward male homosexuals are much more negative than women's attitudes (Ficarrotto, 1990; Black and Stevenson, 1984). Heterosexual men often desire more social distance from gay men (Simon, Glassner-Bayerl, and Stratenwerth, 1991; Sigelman et al., 1991). Such intolerance is evidenced by their negative reactions to gays in the U.S. military and in the increasing number of hate crimes, predominantly committed by heterosexual men against gay men (Comstock, 1991; Martin, 1987; Fish and Rye, 1991).[1]

Homophobia is perhaps the last legally and socially acceptable form of discrimination. While we prohibit sexist and racist behavior, as a society we still promote heterosexism. In the United States, it is socially acceptable and legally legitimate for heterosexuals to subordinate homosexuals and to deny them the privileges that heterosexuals take for granted. This is because the social construction of most versions of masculinity, particularly hegemonic masculinity, thrives on homophobia and heterosexism (Herek, 1987). Heterosexuality has become one of the most important, if not the most important, way that men signify being masculine (Lehne, 1989). By showing they are heterosexual, men can still legitimately claim to be more powerful and valuable than at least one last group of people—gay men.

However, men do not devalue gay men only because of their deviant sexual practices but also because of many gay men's deviant gender activities (Connell, Davis, and Dowsett, 1993; Connell, 1992). By subordinating gay men, straight men are also still devaluing the feminine and anything associated with it, such as women and emotions. Moreover, because some gay men are effeminate, they appear to reject traditional masculinity. In doing so, they call into question the natural continuation of heterosexuality, masculinity, and men's power and privilege. Simply put, gay men pose the greatest threat to the gender order (Connell, 1987).

Homosexuality threatens men's power and privilege because most people assume that biological sex determines both sexual desire and gender behavior. Gay men's existence implies that sexuality and masculinity are distinct social practices, rather than essentially biological or psychological conditions. This is important because the legitimacy of male power and privilege rests on the cultural belief in men's superior biology and psychology. According to this belief, men's birthright grants them privileges and power. Hence, unlike women, gay men pose an inside threat to the preservation and legitimation of male power and privilege because by birthright gay men can demand these same privileges and power (Cockburn, 1991). By invalidating the seemingly natural basis of men's masculinity and heterosexuality, gay men also call into question the legitimacy of male power and privilege. In doing so, they upset the preservation of male power and privilege.

Straight men experience much pressure from each other to oppress gay men and so gay men experience many reasons to fear and despise straight men. Straight and gay men who take the risk of being friends put other men's evaluations of them, their self-esteem, and their identities at risk too. During 1994, I interviewed fifty-six gay and straight male friends and engaged in over 100 hours of fieldwork in a gay community. By studying how some gay and straight men wrestle with stereotypes and prejudices to form friendships, I hoped to unravel the relationship between sexuality, gender, and power, which so far has been mostly theoretical. Next, in Chapter 1, I review previous research that speaks to friendships between gay men and straight men.

Chapter 1

Literature Review

In this chapter, I review the literature on men's friendships, emotion, gender, and sexuality, paying particular attention to how and why men enact masculinity with other men.

MEN'S FRIENDSHIPS

It is hard for most gay and straight men to be friends because they have different life issues and interests. Most gay men do not trust most straight men (Simon, Glassner-Bayerl, and Stratenwerth, 1991), and most straight men devalue gay men. Close friendships, where both friends share a high level of trust, intimacy, comfort, and respect, rarely occur between gay and straight men (Berger and Mallon, 1993; Kurdek and Schmitt, 1987).[1] Most gay and straight men who are friends are casual friends (Hays, 1989). They spend limited time together, are not mutually emotionally intimate with one another, and isolate their friendship from the rest of their lives, particularly from the gay community (Peplau, Cochran, and Mays, 1997; Nardi and Sherrod, 1994). These friendships are not significant in either man's life. Most gay men's close friends are other gay men (Nardi and Sherrod, 1990, 1994; Nardi, 1992b). Most straight men's closest friends are other straight men, though they are often closer to women (Nardi, 1992a; Weiss, 1990; Shields, 1987; Sherrod, 1987).

Gay Men's Friendships

Similar to women's friendships (Crawford et al., 1992; Bleiszner and Adams, 1992; Reisman, 1990), gay men often share emotional intimacy, including nurturing and conflictual emotions for one another and vulnerable feelings about themselves, with their gay friends (Nardi and Sherrod, 1990; Nardi, 1992b). They provide and receive emotional support with one another. With their gay friends, gay men openly signify their homosexuality (Chauncey, 1994; Bornstein, 1994). They refer to themselves as gay men, use gay language, and often act feminine (Rodgers, 1972). They often tease each other about being homosexual and pretend to be sexually attracted to each other (Weinberg, 1978). This signifies mutual acceptance, comfort, trust, and respect for each other (Goodwin, 1989). Through interaction in the gay community, gay men learn vocabulary, mannerisms, and humor (Sprague, 1984). In turn, they use language, humor, and mannerisms to signify membership in the gay community (Moon, 1995; Herdt, 1992).

Straight Men's Friendships

Expressing feelings of vulnerability and affection are outside the limits of most straight men's friendships (Nardi, 1992a; Walters, 1994; Sherrod, 1987; see Walker 1994 for an exception). Most straight men express intimacy with each other "covertly" (Swain, 1989). By joking, especially about such sensitive topics as sexuality, straight men show affection, comfort, trust, and respect for each other (Tannen, 1990). Men often express affection and intimacy with friends by doing activities together; when discussing masculine topics such as sports, work, the military, or politics; or by exchanging physical gestures that indicate liking such as handshakes, bear hugs, and slaps on the back (Swain, 1989; Messner, 1992; Weiss, 1990). Most straight men share covert intimacy in gender-validating contexts, such as while playing sports, at work, or when drinking together (Swain, 1989; Bell, 1981). Most straight male friends do not talk about their conflict with each other (Healey and Bell, 1990 cited in Bleiszner and Adams, 1992). While they provide some emotional support for their friends, most straight men lean harder on women, either partners or female friends, for emotional support (Sherrod, 1987; Shields, 1987). The emotional support they do provide one another does not approach what women provide one another (Walters, 1994; Duck and Wright, 1993).

Straight men allow themselves to express vulnerable feelings about themselves with female friends (Snell, 1989; Williams, 1985). A man will not tell his female friend when he is angry with her, but he will express affection for her (Healey and Bell, 1990 cited in Bleiszner and Adams, 1992). Such friends do not share emotional intimacy equally, however (Buhrke and Fuqua, 1987). Women in cross-sex friendship provide more emotional support than men do, and see their male friends as inept at providing emotional support for them (Buhrke and Fuqua, 1987). Most women in these friendships believe their male friends devalue the emotion work they do (Hochschild, 1983, 1989; Shields, 1987). Hence, women feel less satisfied with these friendships than men do, and value these friendships less (Bleiszner and Adams, 1992).

MEN AND EMOTIONS

Straight men are more emotionally expressive with women and lean more on them for emotional support because women's evaluations of men do not influence their social status as much as other men's evaluations do (Seidler, 1992). Men's competence and acceptance as a member of the gender "men" by other men depends partly on displaying appropriate emotions (Lewis, 1978; Sattel, 1976).[2] By appearing rational and emotionally inexpressive men present an image of self-control and ability to compete with other men (Seidler, 1989, 1991a; Brod, 1987). This can help them maintain status in a situation with men of equal, greater, or lesser status.

Expressing nurturing emotions such as love, affection, and concern may make a man vulnerable to other men, who may interpret a loss of emotional control as "a sign of weakness and an opportunity to secure advantage" (Sattel, 1976:475). Expressing conflictual emotions such as anger, disappointment, or frustration can be dangerous because it reveals information about self that others can use to plan attack strategy. It reveals what is important to a man and what others can do to get to him (Gordon, 1990). The best strategy is to not show any emotion. Emotional restraint "confers power on men, in large part, by effectively withholding information about oneself" (Brod, 1987:8).

To appropriately express emotions we engage in a form of impression management called emotion work or emotion management (Goffman, 1967; Hochschild, 1979). Doing so enables us to avoid shame and "save face." It allows us to present a self that others will positively evaluate and from which we can derive pride (Scheff, 1988, 1990a,b).[3] People do emotion work to evoke an emotion they should experience or express, or to suppress an emotion they should experience or express (Hochschild, 1979; Shott, 1979; Smith and Kleinman, 1989). People can do emotion work for themselves or for others (Albas and Albas, 1988). People can do emotion work verbally, physically, by engaging in social activity, or by offering or denying material objects, assistance, or nurturance (Hochschild, 1979).[4]

Besides doing emotion work to save one's face or status in a situation, a man might do emotion work to acknowledge a lower position or to comply or defer to another's superior position. For example, by expressing shame or embarrassment a man signifies his lower position in a hierarchy (Tannen, 1990; Scheff, 1988, 1990a; Goffman, 1967). Black men's "cool pose" (Majors, 1989) is an example of men doing emotion work to express deference. Black men's expression of disrespect, frustration, and embitterment toward white men marks their subordinate position. Men might also manage another man's emotions to maintain or gain power and position (Kemper, 1990; Flam, 1990; Zurcher, 1982, 1985). They might express negative emotions or withhold positive emotions to intimidate and induce fear or shame in the other man (Clark, 1990; Messner, 1992). By withholding positive emotions, such as appreciation, a man may covertly deny the importance of another man, and make the other feel insecure, less valuable, and/or subordinate (Seidler, 1992; Tannen, 1990). A man might do the opposite and express positive emotions or withhold negative emotions to induce another man's approval (Clark, 1990). Overall, men manage their own and other men's emotional expression to signify masculinity and protect or assert themselves with other men (Weiss, 1990; Seidler, 1989).

GENDER

Masculinity refers to the stylized actions that signify the gender "man" in a given community and time (Schwalbe, 1992).[5] Schwalbe

summarizes this process: To be a man a person must first be identified by others as a member of the male sex category. Then he must
act out the behaviors associated with being male. Then others must
assess his behavior as appropriate; they must infer masculinity from
it. As this illustration shows, gender is both an identity and a behavior (Lorber and Farrell, 1991). Gender is an identity in the sense that
it is a meaning and location for self in relation to others. It is a
behavior in that we signify our identity to others through our actions.

People tend to know and situate themselves in relation to people
who appear similar to them (Ridgeway, 1992; Burt, 1982). One
similarity is sex category membership, male or female. After establishing sex category membership, people display social characteristics and engage in behaviors associated with the assigned sex category. In most communities there are distinct cultural and normative
meanings and practices associated with the male and the female sex
categories (Lorber and Farrell, 1991). While people often determine
others' sex category membership by physical appearance, people
can also engage in sex-identifying displays so that others will categorize them correctly (Ridgeway, 1992). West and Zimmerman
(1987) refer to this process as "doing gender." I will call it "signifying gender." By signifying gender, we present a self to others. Our
display reflects how we think and feel about our selves. It shows
others who we are, how we will behave, what to expect from us, and
what we expect from them (Goffman, 1976).

Signifying gender is always subject to other's evaluations (West
and Zimmerman, 1987; Goffman, 1976). People, in copresence,
assess the appropriateness of others' gender enactments for a given
situation. In general, if a person enacts the characteristics and behaviors sociohistorically associated with their assigned sex category,
then he/she does or displays gender appropriately. Gender assess-
ment may take place regardless of how well a person signifies gender
or even if the person does so at all. Overall, gender identity is an
accomplishment (Lorber and Farrell, 1991; West and Zimmerman,
1987).

Why People Signify Gender

To signify gender a person must not only know how to do so, but
also be motivated to do so. Many conditions motivate people. One,

from an early age, people learn to stake their sense of identity on being a man or woman and to derive self-esteem, efficacy and coherence by being a man or woman (Schwalbe, 1992). Two, self-esteem also derives, in part, from reflected appraisals (Scheff, 1988, 1990a,b). People feel self-esteem when they perceive others' love, acceptance, and approval. By signifying gender appropriately, we demonstrate competence to others, which opens the door to receive acceptance, approval, and love from others. People perceive and label people who do not signify gender, or who do so inappropriately, as incompetent or deviant, and often avoid them.

Three, people shape their behavioral choices by comparing self to similar others (Ridgeway, 1991; Burt, 1982). Men look to other men to determine what identities and behaviors are within their normative parameters of action (Risman, 1992). Men see most other men signifying gender, so that becomes the set of behaviors from which they choose. Four, through gender socialization and from living in a world shaped by gender, people's knowledge, preferences, and observations become gendered (Morgan and Schwalbe, 1990; Morgan, 1992). People have the option of enacting alternative identities and behaviors but to do so they must first imagine the option and then choose to enact it. When people's observations, preferences, and knowledge are gendered they do not conceive of, see, or choose such alternatives.

Five, in a society, people need to be able to interact with others, which requires that people negotiate their action with others (Blumer, 1969). To decide how to negotiate, people need information about others. This information enables them to define others, the situation, and their own situated identity—all of which are necessary for social action. People need a simple way to categorize others so they can make these definitions quickly and begin meaningful interaction. The simplest way is sex. Race, class, sexuality, and religion are others. As we repeat sex-based interaction, we come to expect them. As time passes, our expectations for sex-based interaction become social or gender rules (Connell, 1987). People, then, can just draw on the rule and interaction occurs even quicker. Given this context, people choose to signify gender because it facilitates interaction. Six, given the social utility of signifying gender, over time, groups of people develop structural rewards for doing it and disadvantages for not doing it. For example, higher levels and probabilities of success exist for those who choose to signify gender and who do it well.

Why Gender Is a Problem

Overall, gender provides people with a simple theory or understanding of the world. It provides coherency and consistency and facilitates social interaction. Gender becomes problematic when the material, ideological, and emotional resources for constructing these identities, and the rewards for doing so, differ unequally between men and women (Schwalbe, 1992; Ridgeway, 1992; Kimmel, 1992). Specifically, gender becomes a problem under five conditions: when by signifying gender (1) one gender becomes more highly valued; (2) one gender has better access to and more likely possession of social, political, and economic goods, privileges, and power; (3) men and women come to unequally value those goods, privileges, and power; (4) one gender learns more sources of self-esteem and efficacy; and (5) men and women learn to value the different mechanisms for deriving self-esteem and efficacy unequally.

More generally, gender is problematic in the context of patriarchy. Patriarchy exists when men systematically receive more social, economic, and political resources, opportunities, and privileges than women, and have greater control over the mechanisms by which we distribute these resources, opportunities, and privileges (Acker, 1990; Reskin, 1988; Walby, 1990). Over time, our actions ingrain these differential resources and rewards into our rules for social interaction. They become a part of our social fabric, organizing our behavior and shaping our values. We come to expect and assume that men are entitled to power and privilege because of their sex. We come to see men as having superior biology and psychology; and, hence, see their socially granted power and privilege as natural and right. Over time, then, patriarchy comes to structure or order every aspect of life. Under these conditions, signifying gender becomes a mechanism for the reproduction of gender inequality. Connell (1987) refers to this process and outcome of unequal privileges, power, and resources as the "gender order."

However, while patriarchy or the gender order joins men it also divides them (Connell, 1987; Cockburn, 1991; Segal, 1990). To keep or gain the finite amount of resources and privileges that exist or that they can create, men must compete with other similarly entitled persons. Ironically, the gender order ensures that men's greatest threat to the power and privilege it grants them comes from other men, not women.

MEN DOING GENDER

Given that "being a man" is highly valued in a patriarchal context, signifying gender with other men becomes one way for men to compete for power, privileges, and resources (Kimmel, 1992). As explained earlier, men come to value self and other men for their ability to be a "man" (Schwalbe, 1992). In any given situation, men assess their masculinity in relation to other men and strategize actions based on those assessments (Cockburn, 1983; Stoltenberg, 1989). Through this process they gain a sense of self-worth and relative standing. Hence, many men see interactions with other men as "character contests" (Goffman, 1967), stages on which to assert their masculinity. Those who assert their masculinity the best receive the highest regard, and accordingly, the most power and privilege among the men in the interaction (Morgan, 1992).

Research shows that the motivation to signify one's gender identity becomes heightened when men are with men, whereas women tend to signify gender similarly across situations. Further, groups of men more consistently establish hierarchies than groups of women (Sell, Griffith, and Wilson, 1993; Aries, 1976) and men worry more about their positions relative to other men than women do to other women (Schwalbe and Staples, 1991).

Hegemonic Masculinity

The culturally ideal or "hegemonic" way that men signify being men in the United States today is to (1) display an ability to control, compete, and produce relative to other men, particularly at work; (2) subordinate women and reject effeminacy; and (3) express heterosexual desire (Connell, 1995; Donaldson, 1993; Lehne, 1989; Herek, 1987). Being physically fit and of moderate size also help men to signify masculinity. The better or more a man demonstrates some or all of the above characteristics, the more masculine he seems to himself and to others. Failure to demonstrate some or all of the above characteristics becomes the grounds for men to devalue another man (Morgan, 1992).

Although men of different color, age, ethnicity, and social class in the United States bring unique experiences and meanings to their gender identity, which may or may not blend with hegemonic masculinity (Clatterbaugh, 1990), they are all, by being members of this society, encouraged to internalize hegemonic expectations (Segal, 1990; Brittan, 1989). Men experience pressure from other men not to oppose or resist hegemonic masculinity because doing so threatens all men's access to these benefits (Carrigan, Connell, and Lee, 1985; Reskin, 1988). Subsequently, while men may not agree with all the values and principles of hegemonic masculinity, they, as Bird (1996:130) points out, "often go along with hegemonic norms in order to avoid being pecked." They relegate their nonhegemonic expressions to interactions with women and nonhegemonic men. Their nonhegemonic efforts are not yet collective or ongoing. Moreover, most men find that there are few alternatives that are as socially, politically, or economically rewarding as hegemonic masculinity. Men who oppose or resist hegemonic masculinity are punished. They must give up mainstream positions of success or even survival and forgo patriarchal benefits (Messner, 1992).

Despite these constraints, some men do consistently and enduringly oppose and resist hegemonic masculinity, modifying their expression of masculinity around their social, economic, and political contexts (Connell, 1990a, 1991, 1992; Cockburn, 1991; Stoltenberg, 1989). Some men, such as black men living in ghettos, do this because they are cut off from enacting the basic aspects of hegemonic masculinity, such as holding a "good job." Other men, such as gay men and feminist men, construct alternative masculinities because they do not agree with the basic tenets of hegemonic masculinity.

None of these "alternative" masculinities have changed the gender order, however, because hegemonic men, who hold positions of greater power and influence, marginalize these alternative meanings and deny them cultural legitimacy (Connell, 1995; Bird, 1996). Facing limited opportunities and resources, black men place increased importance on other aspects of masculinity that they can successfully enact, such as physical presence (Majors, 1989). Constructing masculinity in this fashion allows these men to prove their manhood, despite devaluation. In doing so though, they reinforce their subordinate positions; solidifying higher positions for more advantaged men (Messner, 1989).

Masculinity and Homosexuality

Gay men are perhaps the most blatantly subordinated group of men today (Stoltenberg, 1989). They are also the one group of men who have most collectively and enduringly practiced an alternative masculinity that contests hegemonic masculinity on two major fronts: (1) they do not reject effeminacy, and (2) they identify with women (Herdt, 1992; Callender and Kochems, 1985; Bornstein, 1994).[6] As such, they are uniquely situated to change the gender order (Dowsett, 1993; Cockburn, 1991).

Heterosexual men react against this threat by devaluing and ostracizing gay men. They marginalize gay masculinity by deeming it effeminate and, hence, not masculine (Donaldson, 1993). In a culture that values "male" and "masculine" over "female" and "feminine," being effeminate translates into being devalued (Connell, Davis, and Dowsett, 1993; Connell, 1992). Heterosexual men's devaluation of gay men has become a defining characteristic of hegemonic masculinity. Men prove their manhood by displaying heterosexual desire and virility, and by subordinating gay men.

Research has well established that men's attitudes toward gay men are much more negative than women's, and they are much more negative than their attitudes toward lesbians (Ficarrotto, 1990; Black and Stevenson, 1984).[7] Heterosexual men desire more social distance from gay men. Their intolerance of gay men is increasing, as shown by their negative reactions to gays in the U.S. military and in the increasing number of hate crimes committed by heterosexual men against gay men (Herek, 1989).

It is here that we see how heterosexual men's subordination and devaluation of gay men reinforce gender inequality. By devaluing gay men, heterosexual men devalue the "feminine" and anything associated with it, namely women. Occupying a majority of the socially, economically, and politically powerful positions in U.S. society, heterosexual men can foster widespread belief in this "different" and "unequal" label they assign gay men; thereby culturally legitimizing discrimination against gay men and ensuring high costs for choosing or practicing nonheterosexuality (Rubin, 1993; Warner, 1993). In a context where racism and sexism are politically incorrect, by devaluing gay men, all straight men can legitimately claim more power and value than one last group of people.

Overall, straight men experience much pressure to oppress gay men and gay men experience many reasons to fear and despise straight men (Moon, 1995). Straight and gay men who are friends risk other men's evaluations of them, their self-esteem, and their identities. By examining how some gay and straight men struggle with stereotypes and prejudices to form friendships, I hope to help bridge the division between gay and straight men, a division that feeds gender inequality among men and between men and women. In the next chapter, I review my research methods for studying this topic.

Chapter 2

Methods

To describe my research design, I begin by reporting how I collected my data; what kinds of questions I asked and how I found men to interview. Then I specify what "gay" and "straight" mean in this study. Next I outline how I analyzed my data and introduce the reader to the three groups of friends that my analysis revealed. The chapter ends with a summary of the demographic characteristics of the men and the friendships in the three groups.

DATA COLLECTION

From January through December 1994, I conducted in-depth, open-ended, separate interviews with thirty-two gay men and twenty-four of their straight male friends (number of cases [n] = 56). I obtained the interviews using purposive and snowball sampling (Watters and Biernacki, 1989). I identified gay men who had straight friends by networking in a rural southeastern university town. I established access to the gay community via a key informant.

Through the key informant, I made presentations to two gay support groups about homophobia and heterosexism among straight men and women. One was a community group consisting of adult men, and the other was a university group consisting mostly of students. I closed by telling them about my study and requested volunteers from the audience. I handed out a flyer with my name, phone number, and a brief description of my study, for the men to pass on to other eligible gay men. I also contacted a university psychiatrist who ran a closed therapy group for queer people.[1] Though the psychiatrist did not permit me to attend these meetings, she did announce my request for volunteers and distributed my flyer.

I located the straight friends through the gay men. At the end of each interview with a gay man, I requested an interview with his straight friend. I gave the gay man my name and phone number and a brief description of my study to pass on to his straight friend and to other gay men. A week after the interview, I began calling the gay man asking for his straight friend's phone number and the names and numbers of any other gay men with a straight male friend.

For some of the gay men I was not able to speak with the straight friend because he lived out of state (n = 6), was ill (n = 1), or was deceased (n = 1). The out-of-state friends' schedules and circumstances did not permit telephone interviews. For example, one man worked on the road as an entertainer, another man was a medical resident, and another man was a new military recruit. For most of the gay men, the straight man I interviewed is either their only straight male friend or their closest friend (defined by the gay man). A few of the gay men have two close straight male friends; for three of them I interviewed both of their close straight male friends. All in all, I have data on forty-four friendship pairs.

Interviews

My interview guides, one for the gay men and one for the straight men, evolved over the first nine months of the study period (Mishler, 1984). Appendixes A and B contain the final versions. I developed my initial interview guide from reading previous studies on men's friendships. I wrote the questions to elicit the men's accounts of how they deal with sexual differences in their friendship. I inquired about good times and bad times to draw attention to critical events in the friendship (Gergen, 1988). I pretested the initial interview guide with a gay friend of mine and, subsequently, modified the interview questions and my interviewing style.

Once in the field, the guides changed based on (1) comments from the men I interviewed, (2) my reflections on which questions worked, (3) questions that emerged from the interviews, and (4) advice from colleagues. After obtaining informed consent (Appendix C), I taped and transcribed each interview (Appendix D), which lasted between one and two hours, with most lasting an hour and a half. I wrote interview notes after completing each interview.

A week after the interview, I began calling the interviewees asking for the names of additional friends, but also to do follow-up interviews. During these phone conversations the men often gave me new information about themselves, their friends, and their friendships, which I recorded in my interview notes. I did a second face-to-face interview with one gay man and one straight man (not in the same friendship) because they had new stories to share with me about their friendships. I did one joint interview between friends and I interviewed one gay couple together who told me about their independent friendships with two straight men.

Observation

Four months into the study period, the manager of the local gay bar granted me permission to solicit volunteers for my study in the bar. I hung two signs advertising my study in the bar. For the next six months, I went two or three nights a week. I talked to people, got volunteers, obtained follow-up information on men I had already interviewed, and gained background information on men I eventually interviewed.[2]

My participation with an activist group began six months into the study period. During a follow-up phone call, one of my interviewees told me he and another man were starting an activist group and suggested that I come to the meeting. During the first organizational meeting, I identified myself and my research and offered to help with a survey of the gay community. Over the next two years, I became very involved in the group. I contributed to the monthly newsletter, helped organized events, and attended weekly meetings.

While the immediate goal of my observational research was to obtain interviews, it also helped me to better understand the gay community, gay men's lives, and the significance of their friendships with straight men. Many of the gay men shared additional information about themselves, their friends, and their friendships with me during evenings at a gay bar, during support group and gay pride meetings, and at gay social events. Between January of 1994 and September of 1996, I logged over 100 hours of observation, much of which I documented in field notes. I did not write field notes on my work with the activist group. I did not feel it was appropriate, as I did not want to be studying the people I was working with and with whom I was becoming friends. However, these interactions made significant contributions to my understanding of gay men's lives and their friendships with straight men.

Designating Sexual Identity

Sexuality reflects sexual desire, sexual behavior, and sexual identity (Klassen, Williams, and Levitt, 1989; Smith, 1991). Our sexual desire, behavior, and identity are not always consistent with each other (Laumann, et al., 1994). Some statistics demonstrate this point. About 4 to 6.5 percent of U.S. residents have had same-sex experiences in the last five years but do not necessarily identify themselves as homosexual (Binson et al., 1995). A higher percentage of people, about 10 percent of men and 8.6 percent of women, have homosexual desire *or* homosexual behavior *or* identify themselves as homosexual, but not all three (Laumann et al., 1994). Further, it is very common for men who identify themselves as "gay" and "straight" to feel bisexual desire.

Besides not being consistent with each other, our sexual desire, behavior, and identity do not always stay the same over our lives. Some people at some point in life consider themselves to be homosexual, experiencing homosexual desire and expressing homosexual behavior, but later come to identify themselves as heterosexual (Billy et al., 1993; Doll et al., 1992; Fay et al., 1989). Likewise, some people at some point consider themselves to be heterosexual, experiencing heterosexual desire and expressing heterosexual behavior, but later come to identify themselves as homosexual. Other people's sexual desire, behavior, and identity change throughout their lives.

Given the complexity of sexual identity, it was virtually impossible for me to screen out men who (1) at some point in their life experienced or expressed a different sexual desire than they do now, or (2) currently experience but do not express bisexual desire. I only interviewed gay men who, based on their description during our initial conversation, lead predominantly gay lives. They may feel bisexual desire, but they rarely, if ever, engage in bisexual behavior. Furthermore, during our interviews, several of the gay and straight men revealed that the straight men either now or in the past felt different sexual desire than they do now, and some engaged in different sexual behavior in the past. I discuss past and present deviations from the straight men's current identity in the following chapters.

DATA ANALYSIS

I analyzed my data over six steps, guided by the methods of Miles and Huberman (1994). Trying to gain some preliminary understanding of my data, I began by reviewing my transcribed interviews, interview notes, and field notes. I identified all the stories on friendships between gay and straight men for which I had substantial information (n = 44).

In the second step, I treated each friendship story as a case and began looking for emerging patterns in the cases (Bell, 1988). I could tell that the way the men perceive and respond to their sexual differences influences how close they are and how significant the friendships are in the men's lives. Table 2.1 presents a matrix of these dynamics. In some friendships both men accept and respect each other, which allows them to feel very comfortable with each other. These men embrace their differences. In other friendships, while they accept each other, they both do not respect each other's sexual identity, which makes them mildly uncomfortable with each other. These men ignore their differences. And, in some friendships, one or both men neither accept nor respect each other's sexual identity, which makes them very uncomfortable with each other. These men struggle with their differences.

In the third step, I grouped the friendships into three categories above and began thoroughly exploring my data, comparing and contrasting within and between the groups (Yin, 1984). From this process, I discovered that the three groups of friends differ on other important characteristics: (1) how they spend time together, (2) how the gay

TABLE 2.1. Defining Group Dynamics

	Embrace Differences	Ignore Differences	Struggle with Differences
Accept Differences	Yes	Yes	No
Respect Differences	Yes	No	No

man expresses homosexual affection with his friend, (3) whether they spend time with each other's partner, family, and friends, (4) how emotionally intimate they are, (5) how important the friendship is to them, and (6) the sexual tensions and problems between them. Below I introduce the three groups.

Embracing Differences

These friends (n = 13 pairs) are very comfortable with their sexual differences. Both men respect each other's sexuality. They express their sexuality in front of each other, but no more or less than they would with their same-sexual friends. They spend time together often. Both men share emotional intimacy and trust with one another. They embed their lives in one another's. They frequently spend time with both men's partners, friends, and families. In the past, a few of the friends had a sexual experience together. None of them are currently lovers. These men are close, often best friends. Their friendship plays a significant role in both men's lives.

Ignoring Differences

In these friendships (n = 14 pairs) one or both of the men are mildly uncomfortable with their sexual differences. These friends carry on their friendship by ignoring and hiding their sexual differences. Most of the gay men do not feel comfortable showing or talking about homosexuality with their straight friends. While they accept their friends' sexuality, many of the straight men secretly do not respect their friends' sexuality. They do not talk about sexuality, and the gay man does not express his sexuality while with his straight friend. Some of the gay men and many of the straight men share their feelings and thoughts about the nonsexual aspects of their lives, but only the straight men share the more personal aspects of themselves or their lives. Most of the friends spend some time together with some of the other people in their lives, but they do not embed their lives in each other's. Both men like each other, and consider each other to be good friends, but they would like each other better if they had the same sexual preference. None of these friends have had sexual experiences together, or sexual feelings for each other.

Struggling with Differences

In these friendships (n = 19 pairs), one or both men are very uncomfortable with their sexual differences. One or both men do not respect or accept each other at all, and they do not hide it. Many of the straight men are completely uncomfortable with the gay men expressing homosexuality when they are together. Regardless, most of the gay men express their sexual identity when they are with their straight friends. These friends rarely have to confront their sexual differences, though, because they do not spend much time together and are not emotionally intimate. About half of these men never have become friends because of their discomfort with their sexual differences. The other half used to be closer friends before the gay man came out to the straight man. There is a great deal of sexual tension between the friends. In many cases, the gay man is in love or is infatuated with the straight man, or the straight man fears that the gay man is in love or is infatuated with him. Either way, these men can not get past their sexual differences. They are all struggling to be friends.

Validating the Groups

In the fourth step, I returned to the literatures on gender, sexuality, friendships, and emotions to see if these three types of friendships made sense (Yin, 1984). The friends who struggle with their differences are like most straight and gay men who do not trust each other and, subsequently, never become friends. Their friendship was an accident. The friends who ignore their differences are like most straight and gay men who are friends. They are casual friends. The friends who embrace their differences are unusual. They are much closer than anything I found in the literature.

Unlike other straight men, for most of the straight men in this group the gay man is their closest male friend. Not coincidentally, I think it is the uniqueness of the straight men in this group that enables these friends to move so far beyond their sexual differences.

Overall, the literatures on gender, sexuality, friendships, and emotions give meaning to all three groups. However, there are more friendships between men who embrace their differences and fewer friendships between men who struggle with their differences than what previous research suggests. I think the discrepant group sizes are due to my research methods. Most researchers studying men's friendships use either a survey or an interview to ask one member of a friendship about the friendship. No other studies on friendships between gay and straight men have included, by design, both men in a friendship. My in-depth interviews with both friends allowed me to see the men and their friendships through both men's eyes, as well as through my own. I saw sides of the men and their friendships that research with only one friend misses. (See Walker, 1994, for more detail on biases in research on emotional intimacy in men's friendships.)

Finding and Documenting Patterns

Having validated my three groups, I moved on to the fifth step of my analysis. Here I tried to answer the questions that having these three groups of friends posed: (1) Why are some friends accepting and respecting of their sexual differences and others are not? (2) Why are some of the friends closer, more emotionally intimate, and more trusting than others? (3) What is it about the men in each group that motivates and enables them to be friends? (4) Most important, how do the friends' sexual differences in each group differently influence their friendships?

I formed an initial coding scheme around these questions. As I systematically coded my data, I clarified the original groupings, discovered new dynamics, and further developed my concepts and thematic outline. This led to changes in my coding scheme, which, in turn, led to recoding the data numerous times. I summarize the final coding scheme below:

1. How they met
2. What they do together and what they talk about
3. What they do with other friends and family members
4. Their personal disclosure with each other
5. Expression of emotions with each other
6. Giving and receiving of emotional support
7. Problems and issues in the friendship
8. Comfort with their own and their friends' sexuality
9. How important the friendships are to each friend

10. How they enact gender in the friendship
11. When and how the gay man came out to the straight man and how the straight man reacted
12. Each man's values and beliefs about gender, sexuality, and humanity, and what he sees his friend's values and beliefs to be
13. Influences on each man's identity, values, and beliefs and what he believes influenced his friend's
14. Demographics

In the final step, following the qualitative analysis techniques described by Miles and Huberman (1994), I systematically searched the segments of coded text, looking for meaningful patterns of similarities and differences among the three groups of friends. The goal of this process was to answer my four main analysis questions identified earlier. I used the qualitative analysis computer program Ethnograph to facilitate this process. While analyzing my data, I began writing about the patterns I found in the three groups, trying to explain them and link them. My writing revealed holes in these patterns and in my explanation of them, leading me to further analyze my data and reconsult literatures.

Finally, I began choosing excerpts to illuminate the patterns that I found and to support the explanation I provided for them. To maintain confidentiality, I substitute aliases for the men's names. Before I present my analysis of each group, I provide some demographic information about the men and the friendships in each group.

GROUP DEMOGRAPHIC CHARACTERISTICS

Table 2.2 presents the sociodemographic characteristics of each group of friends. I will highlight the important similarities and differences between them. All three groups of friends are mostly white. The men in each group are, on average, thirty years old. There are two older gay men, one seventy-four and one sixty-five, both in struggling friendships. The men who are struggling with their differences tend to be less educated and to have been friends for five to seven years less than the friends who embrace or ignore their differences. This could explain why they are struggling to be friends.

More men who embrace or ignore their differences have other friends with different sexual preferences, giving them more experience with the unique issues of these friendships. This may help explain why they have an easier time being friends than those who struggle with their differences. In contrast to the men in other friendships, fewer of the straight men in embracing friendships have children, and fewer of the gay men have partners. With fewer competing interests, the men who embrace their differences may have more time and energy for their friendship, enabling them to become close friends.

TABLE 2.2. Group Sociodemographic Characteristics

	Embrace Differences (n = 13)		Ignore Differences (n = 15)		Struggle with Differences (n = 16)	
	Gay	Straight	Gay	Straight	Gay	Straight
Years of Friendship						
Range	.5 to 32		1 to 38		.5 to 15	
Average	9.1		11		4	
Other Friend	75%	62%	50%	7%	62%	36%
Bisexual Desire	23%	31%	13%	0%	6%	21%
Partner	8%	69%	50%	50%	14%	64%
Children	15%	31%	0%	64%	13%	50%
Age						
Range	21 to 44	19 to 44	20 to 45	22 to 46	20 to 74	21 to 65
Average	32	30	32	29	33	30
White	75%	85%	82%	93%	93%	93%
College Graduate	50%	46%	55%	50%	21%	29%
Occupation						
Professional	46%	20%	47%	40%	6%	17%
Service	31%	50%	13%	13%	50%	58%
Other*	23%	30%	40%	47%	44%	25%

*Other includes students, retired, and unemployed.

Chapter 3

Embracing Differences

Here I describe the friendships in which both men accept and respect their sexual differences (n = 13). In the chapters to follow I will describe the friendships in which the friends accept, but do not respect, each other's sexual identity, and then the friendships in which they neither accept nor respect each other's sexual identity.

Friendship between gay men and straight men who accept and respect their sexual differences are rare. Unlike most cross-sexual friends, these friends have found commonality in their life issues and interests and have become close, even best friends. Unlike most cross-sexual friends, both men in these friendships respect and affirm each other's sexuality. Their sexual identities are no more or less a part of their friendship than they are in each man's life.

The friendships in this group resemble women's friendships and gay men's friendships more so than they do heterosexual men's friendships or friendships between men and women (cross-sex). Unlike most heterosexual men's friendships, but similar to most heterosexual women's friendships and most friendships between gay men, both of the friends in this group confide in each other, express feelings of vulnerability, and express affection for one another. These friendships resemble cross-sex friendships in that the straight man allows himself to do things with his gay friend that are outside the limits of most straight men's friendships. However, unlike cross-sex friendships, but similar to most heterosexual women's friendships and most friendships between gay men, both men share equal intimacy and emotional support, both feel satisfied with the friendship, and both equally value their friendship.

TIME TOGETHER

As reported by both the gay and the straight man in these friendships, most see each other every week and talk on the phone often. Those who live far apart take regular trips to see each other, spending weekends at one another's homes, and call each other regularly. A couple of the friends (n = 2) lived together at some point in their friendship. One pair lives together now.

Both the gay and the straight man in these friendships described themselves as comfortable doing a wide range of activities together, some which acknowledge their sexual identity and some which do not. They do activities commonly associated with both men and women, as well as gender-neutral activities. They go out to eat together. They go to each other's homes for dinner, for parties, or just to hang out and drink, watch television, or rent movies. They talk about sexual and nonsexual issues such as gay rights, world events, politics, and philosophy. They go see movies with straight and gay themes. They go shopping together. They take trips to the beach and to parks together. They attend football and basketball games, and go bowling, camping, and fishing together. They go to gay and straight bars, and to parties hosted by gay and straight people. Sometimes they dance together.

Both the gay and the straight man noted that this friend was an important person in his life and that he treasured the friendship. Many of the men used an analogy of a brother when discussing their friend with me. Both friends described providing instrumental and emotional help to one another. They buy each other gifts, throw birthday parties, fix each other up on dates, borrow each other's cars and clothes. All the friends said they felt or would feel comfortable asking their friend for any type of help. They have helped each other with car repairs, yard sales, and home improvements. Many reported lending each other money, taking each other in during financial crises, and caring for each other in times of physical and emotional illness. For example, when Chris, a gay man dying of AIDS, first became ill, his friend came to live with him:

> Chris: When he found out that I was sick in June of 1990 he was up here by July or August. He was living in Florida. And he moved up here 'cause he thought I would be dead in a

matter of months. So did I. In October when he realized that I wasn't going to die he said, "I don't think you are going to die anytime soon, so I am going back to Florida." 'Cause I mean he had gotten rid of everything and packed it all in and moved it back up here. But he lived with me for four or five months and he was just very, "You all right? You need something, man?" And I could not have been cared for better; he went the extra mile. "Do you need something to drink? Have you eaten today? Do you need me to fix you some Cream of Wheat or something? Have you had any juice? Taken your medicine?" He was my mother. He put a little extra spin on the bottle that would make it that much sweeter.

By their accounts, both men in these friendships respect each other's sexuality. Subsequently, they enjoy talking and joking with each other about sexual and nonsexual issues and personal characteristics. They do not worry whether their friend will interpret their actions as sexual advances. They talk candidly about sex and dating. The gay men often tell their straight friends about gay men whom they recently met or would like to date. All the gay men conveyed feeling comfortable showing homosexual attraction and affection in front of the straight man, and they believe their friends feel comfortable seeing them do so. All the straight men said they feel comfortable seeing their friends express homosexual attraction and affection, and hearing them talk about it. John recalled:

John: At first it was kind of shocking. And even now it is like, "Oh god, Trip does that? Not the Trip that I know. He does that?" A couple of weekends ago he met this guy that he really liked I guess. And Trip had done way too many shots at the bar. And he was kissing this guy. He was all over him. And I've never seen Trip like that. He tells me his little escapades. The boys he meets. He always calls them the boys. And I don't really want to know this but the way Trip talks about it, it is funny. It makes me laugh. It is just another part of Trip that I've grown to like and talk to him about. Like the other night I called him and we were talking and he was telling me about his sex with the guy from the bar [the guy he was kissing], blow by blow details. No pun intended.

As the above excerpt suggests, most of the friends (n = 11) related joking with each other about homosexuality. They tease each other about being homosexual, pretend to be sexually attracted to each other, and banter with each other using gay language. By joking, especially about sensitive topics like sexuality, both friends in this group show affection, comfort, trust, acceptance, and respect for each other, just as gay men do with other gay friends, and as straight men do with other straight male friends.[1]

EMBEDDEDNESS

Both friends reported frequently socializing with each other's partner or date, family members, and other friends. Most of the men (n = 12) said they enjoy these occasions. All the friends who date or who have a partner spend time together with him or her (n = 12). The gay man and the straight man in most of these friendships (n = 10 out of 12) said they get along well with their friend's partner. They go to dinner, movies, and bowling together. They go to gay and straight bars, and to each other's houses. They do very much the same things they do when the two friends are alone together. Both men reported openly and comfortably expressing affection for their date or partner in front of their friend. And, all the men conveyed feeling comfortable seeing their friend do so. Roy illustrated how comfortable both men feel in these friendships:

> Roy: We have kissed in front of him. 'Cause he knows I am gay and he knows what I am about and what I like and he is not judgmental about it. Plus he has been in the bar several times so he has seen that kind of thing. I think maybe when he first went it might have fazed him. But ever since, no.

Most of the friends reported getting together more frequently with the straight man's partner, and depicted their interactions with her as more relaxed than their interactions with the gay man's partner (n = 10 out of 12). Several of the gay men have even become close friends with the straight man's partner. More of the straight men are in long-term relationships than the gay men ($n = 9$, compared to 2 gay men), so both friends have had the opportunity to get closer with the straight man's partner than they have the gay man's dates.

All the friends reported spending time with the straight man's family and friends (most of whom are straight), and most ($n = 9$) reported spending time with the gay man's family and friends (most of whom are gay). According to both the gay man and the straight man in these friendships, both men invite each other to accompany them to social occasions with their other friends and family. These occasions include dinners, parties, and visits at their friends and families' homes, going to community events, tailgating at football games, going out to bars, attending wedding showers and bachelor parties, and coming over to play pick-up basketball. Both friends reported inviting each over when entertaining friends and family at their homes as well. Some ($n = 5$) of the friends have gathered both sets of friends and family members at times, during which everyone seemingly interacted amicably, as recounted by both the gay and the straight man.

Several of the gay men have become close with their friend's family. They consider themselves to be and describe being treated as a member of their friend's family. They have been with their friend during important life events such as births, vacations, re-unions, and deaths. Several of the gay men have been in the friend's wedding and are godparents to his children.

EMOTIONAL COMMUNICATION

The emotional dynamics of these friendships resemble women's friendships and gay men's friendships more so than they do hetero-sexual men's friendships or cross-sex friendships. Their emotional intimacy exceeds reports from other studies on friendships between gay and straight men, as well as that reported in studies of heterosexual men's friendships.

Expressing Emotions

Both the gay man and the straight man in these friendships reported expressing feelings and thoughts about life happenings, everything from the mundane to the monumental, with his friend. The friends talk about their personal joys, dreams, goals, regrets, failures, and losses. They talk about their financial, legal and educational issues, parenthood, friends, and family, and their health. Charles's friend recently talked to him about his wife being pregnant. He thinks she tricked him into getting her pregnant and wanted her to get an abortion. Charles told him, "Hey look, you knew what you were doing. You are a grown man. When you are married that is not the way it works." Dave recently talked to his gay friend about his infant nephew's brush with death:

> Dave: My nephew was born with heart infection. And the arteries in his heart were crossed so he wasn't getting no oxygen in his blood. And this was, I had a hard time with this because I was questioning my higher power. "Why the hell are you doing this? Why? You know why?" I had a real hard time with it. And Ted, we sat down and talked, and he says, "There is a reason for it. And it is not yours to question."

The gay men in all of these friendships have shared their struggles coming out and their frustrations dealing with social stigma with their straight friends. Jack's friend helped him come out to his staff and helped him handle death threats he received afterward:

> Jack: I had gone through several phases of coming out and I was just stuck really in anger and very strong rage and me dealing with a lot of anger and a lot of rage. He really helped mold me into what I am. He would sit and talk to me. I knew [that] if something happened to me, I would have his support. Because that always made things a lot easier. He was real instrumental in me coming out to the staff. He said, "I really think you should tell them. One of the reasons that I am asking you to do this is because you are withdrawing from them and they don't know what they've done and you have got to tell them it is not something they have done." I was like, "Well,

how do you think I should tell this person? Would it be appropriate if I said it this way or should I even tell this person?" And so I started coming out [to them] one by one. When I came out to a professional staff meeting of forty people, he sent me a little note saying, "I'm really proud of you."

Blake's straight friend Henry helped him come out to their friend Tad, another straight man. These three men were best friends throughout college. The gay man came out to the straight man four years after graduating from college. It divided them. The other straight man did not deal well with the gay man being gay, and he did not like that his straight friend was fine with it. The two straight men even got into arguments about it. Henry stood by Blake throughout, and became a mediator between Blake and Tad.

The straight man in these friendships discusses his beliefs and values regarding sexuality and his identity with his gay friend. John clarified:

John: When I first met Trip, I went through some problems. Things that I had to deal with. Like he showed me some gay porn. It showed two men having anal sex on the screen. It was like, "Wow." It was so, I don't want to say brutal, but raw, right there. I only watched it for ten or maybe fifteen minutes or so. It was a real eye-opener to me. I was like, "How does that make me feel? Does it excite me? Does it make me feel any way?" "No." I was like, "Oh, whew [sigh of relief.]" And being around Trip, the way it made me feel at first, knowing that he was gay, and wanting to be his friend, overcoming my own misgivings about gay people and everything, and he was right there. I had some conflicts in my mind about right or wrong. "What is right? What is wrong?" Everyone has always told me that being gay is wrong. And that gay sex is wrong and dirty and nasty. And so I was like, "Well is it really? What is it? What kind of sharing is it?" I was going through that little bit of turmoil, 'cause I am sure I took it more seriously than other people, 'cause I want to figure it out. I want to know why it affects me this way and feels this way. We talked about that.

Both friends talk to each other about the details of their romantic lives, including their feelings of excitement, heartache, and anxiety, as well as their opinions of each other's dates and partners. For example, Trip recently talked to John about wanting to break up with his boyfriend:

> Trip: I tell him just about everything. There really is not much that has gone on in my life lately that he is not aware of. I have been seeing a stand-up comic, Barry, on and off for a few years. I came to realize that I am not as taken with him as I thought I was. It is just not there. I don't want to pursue it anymore. Dealing with that feeling and having to get that across to Barry, I talk to John about it a lot.

Besides showing their affection by spending time with one another, calling each other, and inviting each other to do things, these men express affection for each other verbally, in noncompetitive ways. In this regard these friendships differ from most straight men's friendships in which men only share their feelings for each other "covertly," such as while playing sports, working, or drinking together. As in cross-sex friendships, friendships between women, and friendships between gay men, these friends hug each other, they say "I love you" to each other, and they tell each other how important they are to one another and what they admire in each other.

These friends also tell each other when they are angry, frustrated, or worried about each other. Usually conflict arises because one friend perceives the other as mistreating him or taking their friendship for granted, as is common in intimate relationships (Rawlins, 1992; Tannen, 1990). For example, one night, Abe slept with a man in Monty's bed while Monty was out of town. Abe did not clean up, leaving a condom wrapper, KY jelly, and a "thank you" note in Monty's bedroom. Monty was furious, Abe was ashamed, they talked about it, and Abe agreed to not let it happen again.

Unlike most straight men's friendships and cross-sex friendships, these friends talk about their conflict. Verbalizing their anger and anxiety leads the two friends to negotiate a solution and keeps the conflict from escalating. Chris explained, "If you hadn't said anything to him it would stay inside of you and you'd think 'I will get him next time.' And then you've hurt yourself and him."

Emotional Support

Both men in these friendships provide and receive emotion work. Both friends described listening to each other, giving advice, offering compassion, and challenging and directing each other's thoughts and feelings. Still, in about half of the friendships, the straight man provides more support because the gay man experiences more emotionally intense issues such as coming out, dealing with social stigma, and living with AIDS or HIV (Tanfer, 1993; Odets, 1995; Ostrow and Wren, 1992; Cochran and Mays, 1994).

However, the gay man talks more with his gay friends about his fear, anger, and loss due to AIDS than with his straight friend. The straight man does not know AIDS as the gay man does. He has not seen AIDS strike down one friend after another. The fear of becoming HIV positive does not live in him as it does in gay men. As Roy explained, the straight man can offer compassion but he cannot commiserate:

> Roy: Our conversations don't get real deep. He is like, "Well how many people do you know that are sick?" And I will count up in my mind. And one of his gay friends is sick and he knew it before I did and we talked about it. It kind of devastated me too. I had no idea. And he knew all about it. So he is having to deal with it too. The bad part about it is that everyone in the world is going to have to deal with it at that point. It is going to be that bad. I've lost nineteen friends.

Both friends consider the imbalance of emotional labor in their friendship as appropriate given their relative circumstances. None of the men portrayed their emotion work as devalued, as women often do in their relationships with men.[2] They do not use emotion work to humiliate one another, to demand deference from one another, or as a way to ingratiate one another, as shown in previous research on men and emotions.

The emotional labor in these friendships most closely resembles the way women engage in emotion work in their friendships with other women and the way gay men engage in emotion work with each other. Most heterosexual men do not engage in as much emotion work as these straight men do. Unlike cross-sex friendships, both of these friends practice emotion work, and both are equally adept at it.

SEXUAL CHALLENGES

Being friends with someone with a different sexual preference creates a unique friendship, with unique issues and tensions. They must confront sources of possible tension between them, such as coming out, sexual attraction, and their homophobia and heterosexism. They regularly deal with homophobia and heterosexism from their friends and families, and from strangers and acquaintances. The straight men rarely encounter these issues in their friendships with straight men, and the gay men deal with them differently with their gay friends.

Coming Out

In almost half of these friendships (n = 7) the straight man either knew from other people that his friend was gay before he became friends with him, or he suspected such early in their friendship. The gay man thought the straight man knew. Nonetheless, the gay man in each of these friendships said he had to officially come out to his friend. He could not be friends with someone who was not accepting and comfortable with him, which requires him to be honest and up front about who he is. For these gay men, coming out was not any more stressful than revealing one's middle name.

Those who waited (n = 6), from one to several years, did so because they were uncertain of their own sexual identity. Shortly after coming out to themselves, they came out to their friends. They worried about doing so. These gay men feared rejection. As recounted by both the straight and the gay man in these friendships, all but one of the straight men immediately accepted their friends. The one straight man said that at the time, over twenty years ago, he was angry and hurt that for a year his friend had lied to him and pretended to be someone he was not. The straight man said that within a few months, he realized he was being self-centered. His friend's coming out was about his friend, not him. He became encouraging and affirming of his friend's identity, participating in gay festivals and speaking at gay support groups.

Homophobia and Heterosexism

Although most of the friends now enjoy amicable relations with each other's family and friends, they apparently have not always been stress free. They have had to address if and how to acknowledge the gay man's sexual identity or the nature of their friendship with each other's friends and families. Their decision influences the frequency and the quality of their interaction with these people. Most of the friends (n = 9) experienced homophobia and heterosexism from the straight man's friends and family, and fear and misplaced assumptions from the gay man's friends and family (n = 6). In dealing with the straight man's family and friends, many of the friends have also revealed the straight man's homophobia and heterosexism.

Issues with the Straight Men's Friends and Family

One of the biggest issues for these friends is whether and when to tell the straight man's friends and family that the gay man is gay. If the straight man does not tell his friends and family that his friend is gay, they might unknowingly say something offensive in the gay man's presence. According to both men, the friends work out some understanding of when the straight man should tell someone, and when he should not. On the one hand all the gay men are out in most aspects of their lives. So, the gay men are usually fine with the straight man's friends and family knowing that he is gay. They often assume people will figure it out. Many of the gay men publicly refer to themselves as gay and use gay speech or act femininely, both common signifiers of homosexuality among gay men. Others, who are not as forthcoming about their sexuality, think their sexuality is evident in that they live with a man, do not have a girlfriend, or do not talk about women.

On the other hand, sometimes the gay man wants to be in control of who knows and how they know. Depending on the people and the situation, the gay man may want to tell the people himself, or have the straight man tell them, or not tell them at all. By default, most of the friends follow a "when asked, tell, and then tell me" policy with the straight man's friends and family. Blake and James, men in two different friendships, presented both men's perspectives on this issue:

> Blake: When Henry told people he told me. I mean, or actually I would ask, "Henry, did you tell?" I mean hopefully neither one of them think they have a license to out me around the world. It is really hard to make me mad, but if I was outed to somebody that somebody knew I didn't want to be out with, I would be pissed. My thing is if you tell somebody I want you to tell me. If you tell somebody that I know especially.

> _____

> James: I make no qualms about it. And they make no qualms about it. Because it is pretty obvious, reading people, that Mason is gay to some people.[3] And some people are very uncomfortable with it, others aren't, but once they get to know Mason it is irrelevant I think. And I will tell people from the beginning. If I think they are going to be uncomfortable, and Mason doesn't care if I tell anybody, it is just a little bit easier.

Besides the gay man's wishes, the two friends have to consider the straight man's wishes. Telling his friends and family that he has a gay friend carries some consequences for him too. While straight men do not want to lie to their families, sometimes they fear their families' reactions. In all but one case, the straight man's parents and family members know the gay man's sexuality. Either the straight man told them or they asked the straight man about it. In the other case, the straight man's mother has not asked and until she does neither friend wants to tell her. They are both worried about her reaction. For the most part, all the straight man's family members have accepted or tolerated the gay man's sexuality. In only one case did the straight man's parents react very negatively, forbidding the gay man to see their son (who was eighteen at the time).

The straight men are less anxious about telling their friends than they are their families. Often their friends' acceptance of the gay man serves as a test of their character. Likewise, the way the straight man handles his straight friends' reaction serves as a test of his character. Josh's conversation with his friend demonstrated:

> Josh: You are going to have to be stronger than I am because you are going to have to deal with a lot of this stuff that I won't. And I don't want to be an excuse either. And I don't want you to use your girlfriend as an excuse every time somebody asks. I don't want that. Either you can or you can't say, "Yes, this is my friend. And that's that."

As related by both the gay and the straight man in these friendships, many friends have endured both unintentional and intentional expressions of homophobia and heterosexism by the straight man's family and friends (n = 9). Ordinarily, the straight man's family and friends act pleasantly around the gay man. Then, later, when the gay man is not present, they share their real opinions about homosexuality and the two men's friendship. Trip and John's experience is a good example. Trip had dinner with John's family. They knew he was gay. John's mother noted that Trip looked unhealthy, implying that she thought he was ill, because she assumed that, being gay, he must have AIDS. The irony here is that Trip exudes fitness. He teaches yoga. Afterward, John's family interrogated John, saying things such as, "We don't know you anymore" and, "We are afraid you are turning gay. Are you gay?"

As Trip and John described, sometimes the straight man's family and friends unknowingly reveal their prejudices in front of the gay man by asking questions about the gay man's health, making negative comments about gay people, or refusing to make eye contact with the gay man. Other times they reveal their prejudices deliberately, intentionally angering and hurting the gay man, and putting the straight man in awkward situations. For example, Charles fought with his straight friend's friend after he uttered negative comments about Charles's sexual identity. One time while Roy and Ron were out together, a friend of Ron's came up to Roy and called him a freak. He asked Ron, in front of Roy, if he knew that Roy "was sweet."

The straight man usually finds these predicaments more distressing than the gay man. To their credit, many of the straight men recounted changing their friends' and family members' prejudices by putting a face on the issue, setting an example for them, asking them why they think as they do, and telling them why they think they are wrong.

Issues About Homosexual Affection

Another big issue in these friendships concerns appropriate behavior with the straight man's friends and family, and sometimes with the straight man himself. The straight man in each of the friendships illustrated that he feels comfortable seeing his friend express homosexual affection, and so does, he attests, his wife or girlfriend. But, he does not want his children seeing or hearing about homosexual behavior. He does not want his children to see his gay friend kiss or hold hands with his boyfriend. He is also aware that many of his other friends and family members do not want to see or hear about homosexual behavior. The straight man cannot avoid this problem by not inviting his friend's lover or partner. The invitation tests how comfortable and accepting he really is, and how good a friend he really is. Not inviting the gay man's date or partner would hurt the gay man's feelings. Blake conveyed the delicacy of this issue:

> Blake: Actually I had a great experience at Henry's wedding. I did really, truly appreciate that he did expressly invite me to bring a date. Because he had a dinner get-together and he didn't invite Sloan. But it is not like he made a point of not inviting Sloan. He just didn't say, "Bring Sloan." And I kind of was bothered by that and I even considered mentioning it to him because I could. Or I considered maybe not going. I just really felt he should have mentioned Sloan. Maybe he didn't realize how serious Sloan and I were. I don't know. Maybe he didn't have a frame of reference for when he should start inviting me to bring dates. And I even made a joke about inviting a date to his wedding. And he goes, "You can do that if you want." Of course I didn't. Because I wasn't dating anybody so why go through the trouble to be the gay green thumb when it is not even a serious relationship? If I had been, if Sloan and I were still together and he was here, then I would have taken him to the wedding. I mean I would at least have

him come to the wedding. I wouldn't walk around with pink triangles on or anything, and we probably wouldn't have held hands. I am not really into public displays of affection. But I would have wanted him there to watch me in my little suit walking up and down the isle. So I felt open to invite a date—a male date—to the wedding.

Blake and Henry however, like the rest of the friends in this group, never directly discussed the issue of appropriate behavior. The straight man assumes that the gay man will act appropriately. Likewise, the gay man assumes that the straight man knows he will act appropriately. He would take offense if his friend assumed otherwise—as if the gay man acted inappropriately at other times. The gay man said he does not change his behavior, and the straight man said he does not expect his friend to do so. However, though both men may deny it, the gay man does intentionally change, or at least regulates his behavior when with the straight man's family and friends. They refrain from showing homosexual affection or attraction. Sam, a gay man, and James, a straight man, in different friendship, reflected both men's perspectives on this issue:

Sam: I think that I am savvy enough that if I am around their friends I would never be real frank about my lifestyle and I think that keeps the worry down a whole lot. I mean, after this many years it is like sonar. I can sense the situation I am in and know where to go and what to do and what not to do with it. Gay people are in a constant mode of edit. We edit everything that comes out. You know—oh I am in this situation so I will have to use a pronoun. I don't want to say he. And it is a real stage of edit. So you get to where you are an expert at it. And I would never want to embarrass friends of mine, and it is none of those people's business anyway if they are just casual friends of his, that they even need to interact with me in that way. I think they should just trust me. And if they brought it up I think that would bother me. It is like you decided that I am your friend so you are going to have to trust me that I know how to behave in whatever situation I find myself in.

James: I don't think my kids know. Maybe because we never talked about it. We have never talked about sexuality in that aspect. When Mason is around them, for the most part, he is like anyone else. I mean he is not in drag. He is himself. At this age I think they are a little too young to understand. Mason is a professional person. He works with children. He knows what is appropriate and what is not appropriate. So that would never be a problem in our relationship, I don't think.

As these excerpts show, for now this unspoken expectation for appropriate sexual behavior seems to be working. However, eventually these men will probably have to tackle this issue head on and confront the straight man's heterosexism. Most likely, this will occur as the straight man's children age and become aware of their surroundings.

Issues with the Gay Man's Friends and Family

The friends face a different set of problems with the gay man's family and friends. Although all but one of the gay men are out, like most gay men, they have a few people in their lives from whom they keep their sexual identity a secret—usually select family members and co-workers (Warner, 1993; Troiden, 1988). Subsequently, many straight men have joined their friends in the closet.

The biggest problems the two friends have with the gay man's friends, according to both men, concern whether these other gay people accept the straight man's identity. In many cases the gay man's friends and acquaintances assume that the straight man must really be gay or bisexual (n = 6 out of 9 friends who socialize with the gay men's friends). They cannot accept that a straight man could be friends with a gay man, so they believe he must be a closet queer or maybe he just does not yet know he is gay. Some of the gay men's friends thought the two friends were secret lovers.

The gay man finds these reactions disappointing. He worries that other gay people, making false assumptions, will make advances toward his straight friend or offend him in some way. The gay man's own close gay friends do not hit on the straight man. In several cases (n = 5), though, acquaintances or strangers have hit on the straight man while he was out with the gay man (n = 5). The gay man tries to manage these situations by warning his straight friend about what may happen. For example, Roy told his friend Ron, "All gay people are not like myself. We are all different, of course. There are those that will hit on you no matter what."

The gay man also tries to prevent this behavior by other gay men by telling them "hands off." Sometimes the gay man communicates this message by telling other gay men that the straight man is his date. For example, Josh had his friend with him at a gay bar and another gay man kept hitting on him. So Josh said, "That's my boyfriend. Do you mind?"

While the gay friend worries about these advances, the straight man does not get anxious or angry about them. He does not like being hit on, but he tries to take the attention as a compliment. For example, one night at a gay bar, several men grabbed Ron's butt and several others came up to him and said, "Mmm." He took a positive angle: "It was the first bar I had ever been to where I knew I could get laid. No doubt in my mind." None of the straight men reported feeling threatened by these advances. The way they see it, no one can make you have sex with them if you do not want to, unless they force you. None of the straight men fear rape. They all feel confident they could protect themselves. Dave and James, two straight men, elaborated:

> Dave: Well you can see I am not a small boy. If it really came down and they get pushy with it I could thump them in the head. I have no qualms with that. I am a construction worker. I have been in a few scraps before. It is no problem.

> ───────────

> James: Nobody is going to do anything to you if you don't let them or encourage them to do it. If someone touches you inappropriately, which may happen—a woman may do it— you simply say, "I don't appreciate that."

Once the gay man's friends accept the straight man's identity, many of them became uneasy around him for a while. Gay people are often protective of their communities and need proof before trusting an outsider (Chauncey, 1994; Kennedy and Davis, 1993;

Herdt, 1992). With time the straight men prove their sincerity to the gay man's friends and socialize with them frequently. The road to that point was a bit bumpy for most of the straight men. For example, Ron said one time he told a gay joke with his friend's gay friends and they did not laugh. He felt bad, though he understood their reaction. Another straight man, an American Indian named James, explained why the tensions exist:

> James: I think sometimes in the gay community they have their own prejudices too. Everybody tries to stereotype everybody. I mean how many times have I gone into a school and some kid asks me do I live in a tepee. So I think in each subgroup people have stereotypes and they begin to believe them. There is a lot of intolerance in the gay community too where a lot of them don't want to associate with heterosexuals.

Strangers and Acquaintances

The gay man worries that people will assume his friend is gay because he socializes with a gay man. More specifically, he worries that this will make his friend angry or scared, and his friend will abandon the friendship. The straight man, though, reportedly does not care if people think he is gay. He might tell them otherwise but if they do not believe him, who cares? It was something he worried about when he was younger, but it does not matter now. What matters is their friendship. From the straight man's perspective, those people have a problem, not him or his friend.

In some cases (n = 3), the straight man's casual friends and acquaintances ridicule him for being friends with a gay man. He does not feel threatened, though. Nor does he subsequently distance himself from his gay friend. Several of the straight men have confronted strangers about being heterosexist, even when not with their gay friends. For example, James scolded his co-workers for ridiculing another co-worker for being gay; his neighbor for thinking gay people are unfit to teach in grade school; and his brother-in-law for wanting to exclude gays from the military. And John recently confronted two men at a jazz bar who were harassing a gay couple:

> John: There were these really sweet, black, gay men, older, silver hair, looks like they were on a date, very much enjoying

the music, and the ambience, and the food and wine. And
Mavis [his fiancee] and I kind of picked them out. They were
not overtly homosexual at all. And it was so cute 'cause every
now and then one of them reached over and touched the other's hand. And it was really cute. And, not that color has
anything to do with it, but there was a group of four, two black
guys and two black girls dressed like Queen Latifah [a famous
female rap musician] and they were drinking, and the two old
men finished their coffees and got up to leave. This was a very
nice place. Not the type of place you do this. And one of the
black guys goes, "See ya, girls," really loud. I turned around,
and I said, "Why don't you have some respect for yourself and
for others? Act like you have some class." He didn't like that
at all. So he started mouthing off to me. "I'm 6'2", 200
pounds, and I will kick your ass." I said, "You're 6'2", 200
pounds, but it is probably all fat, chump. Why don't you come
over here?" I said that very low so no one else could hear me.
He kept getting louder and louder. I wasn't provoking him but
I wasn't going to back down from him either 'cause it really
pissed me off what he said. I wanted to say something about it
'cause it just wasn't right. It ended up that he kept it up and
was asked to leave by a manager. And he calmed down.

The straight man worries about the gay man being harassed in his
presence. More specifically, he worries about how he will react. He
imagines harassment scenarios. He envisions himself defending his
friend, if necessary. The gay man, though, said he does not worry
about strangers harassing him.[4] He has been through it countless
times. He knows all the situational contingencies to his reactions,
which include ignoring the harasser, verbally confronting the harasser, and defending himself physically. Several of the friends
$(n = 6)$ have been together when someone harassed the gay man.
Both friends stood up to the harasser. Others, like Monty and Abe,
have talked about how they will react if it occurs. Monty plans to
defend his friend:

Monty: If we were out in public together and some guy started
talking shit, I would probably take up for him. 'Cause that
ain't right for nobody. That is just like somebody walking by

and they can't help it 'cause they got a mole on their face and somebody saying something.

Eroticism

According to the gay men in these friendships, none of the friends are currently lovers. In the past, two of the thirteen sets of friends had sex together. Two came close. They caressed, kissed, petted, or slept in the same bed, but did not have sex. None of the four straight men involved recounted these experiences to me. It is not unusual for gay men to have sexual relations with men who identify themselves as straight (but are in the closet), but it is rare for them to become or stay friends afterward (Laumann et al., 1994; Billy et al., 1993; Doll et al., 1992; Fay et al., 1989). As told by the gay men, usually one of two situations occurs. In the first situation, soon after they become friends the "straight man" hits on the gay man. The straight man wants to carry on an affair with his new "friend." This scenario did not occur between the friends in this group.

In the second situation, the gay man, not yet out, initiates a conversation with a man whom he finds attractive and whom he senses is gay.[5] The two, presumably straight, men become friends. One man feels sexually attracted to the other but does not act on it. Then, one night, frequently after the friends have been partying, when both men's inhibitions are low, one man, usually the straighter of the two "straight men," initiates sexual contact. This scenario tends to happen in the beginning of the friendship, commonly during late high school or college when the friends were exploring their sexual identity. After the experience, the man who recognized his homosexual attraction earlier comes out to himself and to his friend. The other man, the initiator, who professes innocent sexual curiosity, decides to lead a straight life.

Usually the sexual affair ends the friendship. The straight man does not want reminders of his experiment, or proof that it occurred. In rare cases, as has happened with four of the friends in this group, the friendship survives. Rather than deny their sexual experience, according to the gay man in these friendships, they talk about it. They talk about how it makes them feel, and how they now feel about their friendship. Both men see their friendship as more important than that one night. They agree to put their sexual attraction aside. The gay man silences his feelings for his straight friend by thinking of him as a brother. This seems to work well. In fact, many of the gay men who have not felt any sexual attraction to their straight friends voiced exactly this sentiment. Roy explained that he could not fathom doing anything sexual with his straight friend because it would be like being with one's brother:

> Roy: Once I am friends with someone, it is like me trying to sleep with Jacob (his best gay friend). I would just bust out laughing. 'Cause we are such good friends. And we have talked about it. "Can you imagine us sleeping together?" And both of us just laugh. It would be the same thing. Even though he [Ron] is straight. It would be the same thing to me. I mean we probably both would laugh.

Occasionally, though, according to the gay man in these four cases, the friends reminisce about their past affair. Their past affair has presented unique problems for them over the years. They have had to decide whether to tell their partners about the affair. In two cases, in which they told the partners and the men are still with those partners, the partners (one straight woman and one gay man) are jealous of the two men's friendship. These friends do not enjoy spending time with the jealous partner. This constrains their friendship. The men who are still with the partners that they chose not to tell feel guilty about it to this day, even twenty years later. One gay man feels especially guilty because he is friends with his friend's wife too. He feels as if he cheated on two people, his partner and his friend's partner.

Given the abundance of "not-so-straight" straight men, many of the gay men worried ($n = 5$), in the beginning of the friendship, that the straight man wanted something more than friendship. The gay men in these friendships worried about sending the wrong message to their straight friends. They worried that the straight man would perceive things they said or did as a sexual invitation. Similarly, other gay men worried that their new straight friend would, through the experience of being friends with a gay man, discover some latent homosexual desire and make a sexual advance toward them. For example, one straight man walked in on his gay friend while he was undressing. The gay man worried that his straight friend would suddenly become gay after that experience. He felt very guilty, even though it was a complete accident and totally out of his control. But the straight man was not concerned about it. With time, when none of these fears come true, the gay men stop questioning their friends' motives.

Presently, as discussed earlier, most of the friends, according to both the gay and the straight man, joke and tease each other about homosexual behavior and desire. For example, John and Trip dance together while at a gay bar. They also tease each other about wanting to have sex together. Roy described another example when Ron and Ron's girlfriend staged a surprise striptease for Roy's birthday:

> Roy: At my birthday, I wanted to have a male stripper. And the guy that I wanted to have wouldn't do it. So Dana and them were there and I was getting ready to go out and celebrate my birthday with my friends, and all of a sudden they said, "Don't go anywhere. We will be there in a minute." I was like, "Okay." I figured they had a surprise for me or something. And Chap got up and started stripping. And Dana and Ron were about to die laughing. He got all the way down to a g-string. First he starting ripping his shirt off, I was turning beet red. I could feel myself turning red. And then I dropped my head and started laughing. And he is dancing in front of me saying, "Where are my tips?" I said, "I can't tip you." It was hysterical. Dana, I thought she was going to wet her pants.

By joking around in this manner, the friends reaffirm their mutual acceptance and trust. They show their affection, comfort, and respect for each other, just as gay men commonly do with their gay friends, and straight men do with their straight friends. Neither friend said they worry about their parody becoming reality. None of the friends admitted to presently desiring a sexual relationship with the friend, nor do they worry about the friend making a sexual advance. Art explained:

> Art: I think gay men and straight men miss out when they let sexuality stand in the way of their friendships. I really do. I would take nothing from my relationships with the straight men in my life and there is no way I would ever jeopardize that

relationship in any way. That would diminish it. We joke. We cut up. We have a good time. Straight people cut up about gay people with me. It is nothing demeaning. It is like a heterosexual male having relationships with women. Every relationship does not have to be sexual. And gay people need to learn that as much as straight people, from what I am seeing.

Some of their joking around goes outside liberal boundaries of platonic friendship. Discussing their sex lives explicitly; hugging, touching each other jokingly; reminiscing about their past sexual history—these are all questionably erotic activities (Dowsett, 1993; Miller, 1983). Even though they touch under the pretense of humor, humor often contains seeds of truth (Collinson, 1988; Rommetveit, 1974). This being the case, these friends exemplify how friends can be aware of sexual attraction to each other but not desire a sexual relationship. There is sexual energy between them. This is also true of friendships between heterosexual men and women, and probably friendships between heterosexual men. The friends in this group do not fear the sexual energy between them, as most men would. Because they are not afraid, they can play around with and joke about their sexual energy. They use humor as a vehicle to safely express their sexual attraction or curiosity. This does not make their friendship a romance. It does not make the straight man bisexual or gay. Instead, to me, it shows how comfortable these men are with their own sexual identities.

CONCLUSION

The friends in this group have moved beyond the heterosexism and homophobia that prevent most gay and straight men from becoming friends. These friends respect and trust each other. Both friends are comfortable, accepting, and affirming of each other's sexuality. They allow their sexual differences to enrich their friendship. Most are best friends. They share their thoughts, emotions, and lives with one another. Their intimacy exceeds that found in friendships between most straight men, as well as that found in other friendships between gay and straight men.

Chapter 4

Ignoring Differences

In this chapter, I describe the friendships in which both friends accept each other, but both do not respect each other's sexual identity (n = 15). In about a third of the friendships it is the straight man, in a third it is the gay man, and in another third it is both men. These men are mildly uncomfortable with each other. The gay men do not feel comfortable showing or talking about their sexuality with their straight friends. Likewise, most of the straight men do not or would not feel comfortable seeing their friends express homosexual affection or desire. These friends carry on their friendship by ignoring and hiding their sexual differences. They spend time together with some of the other people in their lives, but do not embed their lives in one another's. Both men consider each other to be good friends, but they would like each other better if they had the same sexual preference.

These friends are more than casual friends, but not as close as those who embrace their differences. Looking at these friendships from the gay man's position, these men's friendships resemble most cross-sexual men's friendships. The two men spend time together only in the "straight world," apart from the gay man's relationships with other gay men and lesbians. Like most gay men, the gay man in each of these friendships does not fully trust his straight friend. He, like most gay men, is consequently much closer to his other gay friends.

Looking at these friendships from the straight man's position, the emotional dynamics resemble those of romantic relationships between men and women and friendships between men and women. The straight man in most of these friendships finds it easier to be emotionally intimate with his gay friend than with his other straight male friends, just as most straight men feel more comfortable being emotionally intimate with women than with their straight male friends. He, like other straight men, finds emotional intimacy with his straight male friends awkward. For several, the gay man is their closest male friend. Like other straight men though, many find their friends' sexual practices unacceptable.

TIME TOGETHER

These friends can talk about almost anything, but understand that they will not talk about the gay man's sexuality. Peter, a gay man, summed up how these friends spend time together:

> Peter: Well, you don't have to talk about gay sexual issues. You know you could talk about anything. They are just friends. It doesn't have to center on a gay theme. Just like, we are two people. We get along. We hit it off. We talk about sports. There are different angles of course, but I mean you talk about what drinks you like, where you like to go for vacation, how bad the job is. That is the main thing definitely. If a gay man can be secure enough in himself that he shares that with somebody that he is friends with and they can accept it, then they are truly, they are really, truly friends. It hardly comes up. We don't even think about it. We don't even think of each other as straight and gay. We just think of each other as Rick and Peter.

As Peter pointed out, these friends do not think of each other as gay or straight. Karl, a straight man, noted that sometimes he forgets that his friend is gay. He tries not to reflect on his friend's sexuality. Similarly, Justin said the only way most friendships between gay and straight men can survive is if the gay men "don't throw their gayness in their friends' face. The more you throw it in people's face the more they'll [be] apt to get tired of that mess and go separate ways."

Like those who embrace their differences, both men in these friendships report seeing each other every week and talking on the phone often. Many of them work together. Many of them live together, or lived together in the past. They do many different activities together. They go shopping, go to concerts, and exercise together. They go to the beach, restaurants, and movies together. Frequently, they hang out at their houses together, watching TV, having dinner together, playing games, drinking, talking about work, school, their mutual friends, music, social issues, sports, and recreational pursuits. Like the friends who embrace their differences, these friends help each other do things and care for each other in times of need. They lend each other money, and give each other a place to stay when they need it. They take care of each other when they are physically or emotionally ill. For example, Mitch's straight friend tried to commit suicide after his wife left him and took his son with her. He showed up at Mitch's home distraught, spent the night, and then for the following year Mitch provided emotional support, covered for him at work, and shared his home with him.

Unlike the friends who embrace their differences, these friends do not do things together in the gay community. In this respect they resemble most cross-sexual men's friendships. Seeing or hearing about homosexual desire makes the straight man uncomfortable. So, they do not go to see gay movies or gay musicians together. They do not go to gay parties or to gay bowling or skating nights. They do not go to gay bars. Some went once and felt intense discomfort. Lane, a straight man, explained, "It is more of a place for them." Trent pointed out that "homosexuality on a grand scale" troubles his straight friend. The straight man's discomfort makes even spending time at the gay man's house problematic for these friends, as Steve voiced:

> Steve: I've gone over [to] his house a few times. We'd known each other for I guess about nine months before I went over to his house the first time. When I went over there the first time I was kind of taken aback because his house is decorated with pictures of naked men and that kind of thing and that was kind of a shock even though I knew he was gay. It was not something that we talked about. So for it to be kind of right out there in front of me and be advertised almost—it was kind of—it made me uneasy for a little bit.

Often, the gay man does not want to go to a gay bar with his friend either. He would feel uncomfortable seeing gay men kissing or dancing or touching each other in front of his straight friend. Having his straight friend around his gay friends is okay because the gay man knows that his gay friends will not act inappropriately. Aaron, who lives with his friend Matt, illustrated this side of the issue:

> Aaron: When he got up here he met his first gay people other than me in his life. And it happened to be a lesbian friend of mine. And they hit it off. Matt is 6'10". He is a huge guy. But he is as gentle as a big bear. And they just have a ball. She will come in and sit in his lap and cuddle and stuff. He got a lot of positive experiences with these gay people—with these girls. Now had it been guys, because of the way he was brought up, I don't think he would have been okay. Since then he has met guys and he doesn't have a problem. He says gay people are hilarious. He thinks they are fun to be around. Because they are weird. And I am comfortable with it. Now I wouldn't take Matt to a gay bar with me. I don't know why. I would take him anywhere else. I don't know if he would feel comfortable. But I wouldn't hesitate to have friends over.

As the excerpts above show, the friends worry about hurting each other's feelings and behaving appropriately with each other. This carries over into how and what they will joke about with each other. They will joke about nonsexual topics, such as what they are wearing, things they say or do, or about other people. However, most do not joke about their sexual identities (n = 12). For example, one would not hear the gay man telling stories about other people trying to set him up with women, or about how awkward weddings can be for him. Neither friend makes fun of his own or his friend's identity by using names such as "sissy," "queen," or "fairy" in jest. Neither friend imitates being a stereotypical effeminate gay man, or an uptight straight man. They rarely tell gay or straight jokes with each other. Steve and the other straight men think this would be disrespectful and might hurt his friend's feelings:

> Steve: There are some girls at school that I think are almost insulting with their jokes about homosexuality. They always make a big issue out of not making it an issue that he is gay, and will kind of announce his homosexuality sometimes when

I feel like it should be his choice. Sometimes it makes me angry. But I've never said anything because I am not going to rescue Jim. It is his life and his sexuality. And if he is okay with it, then I'm fine with it too. But there's been times when I felt like some people stepped over the bounds.

Whereas the friends who embrace their differences use sexual humor to express their comfort with each other, these friends see sexual humor as a liability. The gay man refrains from joking about his own and his friend's sexuality because he thinks it might make his friend uncomfortable. In addition, both believe it would bring attention to a fact that they are trying to ignore—that they have sexual differences. Those gay men who do joke about their sexuality are cautious not to get too personal or too graphic. The straight man rarely intentionally initiates jokes, though he will laugh along with the gay man if the gay man makes a joke. Karl and Lane, two straight men, commented:

> Karl: I don't joke about it that much. He jokes about it more than I do. Telling gay jokes and stuff like that. I might pick on him about something. He might like a particular guy and I will say, "Well so and so called and he wants you to meet him at the hotel." Just messing around. He just starts cracking up.

> ———————

> Lane: I can dish it right back. It is all joking, fun. I know he wouldn't say anything intentionally that would offend me. We really respect each other's feelings. We tease. But respect each other's feelings.

All the friends talk about homosexuality as a social practice, but do not talk specifically about the gay man's homosexuality or his sex life (n = 11). The straight man asks the gay man all the questions he is afraid to ask other men, such as how gay people meet, how do they date, how do they know what to do? These topics are safe to discuss because both friends can put some distance between what "gay people do" and what this particular gay man does. Because homosexual affection disgusts him, the straight man does not want to think specifically of his friend engaging in such activity.

Consequently, the straight man will not ask his gay friend about his personal sex life. Sensing this, Jim and the other gay men do not bring up their sex lives:

> Jim: Guys may say they are comfortable but I don't think they really want to hear you talking about being in love with another guy. They accept the fact that you two are hanging out together and you guys are together but they don't want to hear about it. That is just the feeling I get. They never ask. They may know but they will never ask are you seeing anybody.

The gay man also avoids discussing his personal life because it calls attention to his sexuality and the two friends' sexual differences, which these friends are trying to ignore. For example, Rick talks to Peter about sexual tensions between him and his wife. Rick wants a vasectomy. His wife wants another child. Peter, though, does not talk about anything personal with Rick. It would make both friends uncomfortable:

> Peter: He comes to me with a lot of things. I don't know, I probably wouldn't talk to him in detail about sexual exploits. I just know that there are subjects that he doesn't like to talk about, you know. And there are subjects with me that I don't like to talk about, especially things about my sex life now. I am a very private person.

The gay man in these friendships might mention that he has a date, but he would not say who it was, or where they were going, or how it went. A gay man in a long-term relationship rarely discusses his personal life, such as what he and his partner did over the weekend. The gay man does not show attraction to other men when he is with his straight friend. For example, unlike those who embrace their differences, the gay man in most of these friendships would not say, "Hey, that guy is cute" while walking in the mall with his straight friend. In contrast, according to both friends, the straight man in each friendship talks about his girlfriend, wife, or date. For example, the straight man might talk about a fight he had with his wife over the weekend. Or, expressing excitement, he may ask the gay man to help him plan a date with a woman.

EMBEDDEDNESS

These men do not embed their lives in one another's as much as those who embrace their differences. Most of the friends spend time with mutual friends, but not with their individual friends or families. While most spend time together with the straight man's girlfriend or wife, only a few spend time with the gay man's date or partner.

Partners

As described by both men, about a third (n = 5) of the friends never spend time with either man's partner or date, a third (n = 6) spend time with just the straight man's partner or date, and a third (n = 4) spend time with both men's partners. None spend time together with the gay man's partner without the straight man's partner. Both men feel awkward spending time together with the gay man's partner or date. Everyone feels uptight about expressions of homosexual affection. The gay men are restricting their usual behavior together, so they do not feel like themselves when they are with the straight man. Regardless of how comfortable the straight man truly is, homosexual affection captures his attention. He worries this might make him appear uptight, which might disappoint or embarrass his friend. Jake explained, "It is like those kinds of images are really socially loaded, I think. That surfaces and then I get beyond it. But initially there is like shock value." Steve described a recent trip to a gay bar with his friend Jim and Jim's boyfriend Charles:

> Steve: I think back to the gay bar and I think about how tense I probably looked because I know how tense I felt. And so I wonder if maybe I embarrassed him with Charles. 'Cause I had just met Charles basically. I wonder if I may have been insulting. Or embarrassed him in that way. But you know I asked him about it when we got back. He said, "No, they didn't notice." Whether they truly did and he is just blowing it off I don't know.

Adding to the tension, as with the friends who embrace their differences, the gay man in many of these friendships (n = 6) reported that his partner is jealous of the straight man and distrusts the two men's friendship. The gay man invests or would invest considerable energy into managing his partner's emotions when with his straight friend. One straight man, Karl, who lives with his gay friend, Jack, and Jack's partner Walter, and Jack's straight brother Lane described such a situation:

> Karl: I told Jack that when it was just Lane and Jack and I it was a lot different. It was a lot happier. We used to talk more. Hang out and drink coffee and talk or drink a beer and talk and sit outside. We still do it but as soon as you get in a conversation here comes Walter. And Lane and I will get up and leave. We don't like to even be around the guy. He is conniving. He is real protective, domineering. Anywhere Jack goes he follows him.

Given all the tension, the gay man in many of these friendships finds it much easier to avoid spending time with his friend and his partner together (n = 11). In contrast, according to both men, they get together much more frequently with the straight man's partner. As with the men who embrace their differences, both men in these friendships enjoy spending time with the straight man's partner. Everyone seems relaxed. All the partners (n = 7) of the straight men know of the nature of the two men's friendship. None of the straight men think their partners feel jealous or personally threatened by the gay man. The straight men who are dating (n = 8) usually wait to tell their dates about the nature of their friendship until after they have been dating for a while and until the woman meets the gay friend. Her reaction to the gay friend serves as a litmus test for her compatibility with the straight man. If a woman reacts negatively to him having a gay friend, then he knows this is not the woman for him.

Friends

A couple of the friends (n = 2) will socialize with the straight man's other friends, all of whom are straight. A few (n = 3) will socialize with the gay men's gay friends. A couple (n = 2) will socialize with any of either men's friends. Unlike those who embrace their differences, rarely do any socialize with both sets of friends simultaneously. The men in the remaining friendships (n = 8) do not spend time with each other's friends.

In the cases where the friends socialize with one or both men's other friends (n = 7), the gay man informs all his friends about his friend's sexuality. None of the gay man's friends hit on the straight man, and the gay man does not worry about his friends hitting on the straight man. The straight man worries about interacting with his friend's gay friends. But some, such as Matt, found that the experience helped him accept his friend:

> Matt: We had a real good time, it didn't matter who you were or what you were doing. And she was also a big influence on Aaron 'cause she let him see, "Well, hey, it is okay to be who you are." And she also let me see, "Hey, it is okay for him to be who he is or me be who I am." But him meeting new and different people up here has helped him, which also helped me.

The straight man in these seven friendships worries about how his gay friend and his straight friends will get along. He does not think it is his place to tell his straight friends about his gay friend's sexuality, but he thinks his straight friends will figure it out and will ask him. He does not want to lie to them. The gay man in these friendships would rather come out to them himself, but understands the dilemma his friend faces. So, the friends follow an "if they ask or if they seem to suspect, tell" policy. For example, Grant is going to be in Don's wedding. Don worries about how Grant will get along with the other straight men in the wedding, but is not planning to say anything about Grant's sexuality unless asked. Recently at a prewedding party, one of them asked Don about Grant. Don told him.

Although they do not publicly deny their sexuality, none of these gay men announce their sexuality. Like many gay men, they have not formally come out to everyone in their lives. The gay man expects the straight man to respect this decision. Since most of these friends either work together, go to school or church together, live together, or grew up together, many of the straight men (n = 10) know the other people in their friends' lives. The straight man wants to respect the gay man's decision, but two problems arise. One, he does not always know who knows. Two, he struggles with how to respect his friend's identity and still be friendly with him when they are with other people. Jim, a gay man, and Jake, a straight man, depicted two different perspectives on these situations:

> Jim: It is like you're telling my business. And at the same time I am concerned about it, I don't care about it. Because I don't know them, they don't know me. They can't do anything to hurt me. I don't think they are doing it to hurt me. I think they are just thinking that maybe I am coming out in conversation, 'cause I seem so comfortable about it that they figure I must not care, that it is not a big deal. I actually do, because that is my personal life.

> Jake: In those kind of interactions it is like, say, for example, I have a belief about being open, honest, yet there is somehow a dilemma or a contradiction I face when I am with someone that has that identity and my openness might place their identity at risk. My choice to talk about in, say, a classroom or work setting the fact that someone is gay is problematic, I think. More so than talking about someone being heterosexual. I can talk about my wife in ways that don't put at risk my identity but I can't talk about Sal's partner without putting him at risk. So there are these contradictions that are at work that struggle with that.

The straight man tries to respect his friend's wishes by observing an "if they ask, be vague" policy. If a person asks a question that would reveal the gay man's sexual preference, the straight man answers honestly, but provides no details. Or, he will tell the individual to ask the gay man. It can get tricky, especially with people who suspect the gay man is gay. These people sometimes persistently question the straight man about it. Still others question the straight man's sexuality since he is friends with a man whom they suspect is gay. A woman once turned down Tom, a straight man, for a date because she thought Tom was gay since he was friends with Cory, a man she suspected was gay. In another example, Steve's co-worker told him she thought he was gay because of his friendship with Jim, a man she suspected was gay. Besides managing his friend's sexual identity, the straight man often has to defend his own.

Family

Managing his secret with his own family and friends does not stress the gay man. Identity management has become a habitual part of daily life for many gay men. However, managing the gay man's secret with the straight man's family produces considerable anxiety for both men. Subsequently, according to both men, half of the friends (n = 7) do not spend time together with either of their families, and those who do (n = 8) keep the gay man's sexual identity quiet while with them. Two of the sets of friends will spend time with the gay man's family but not the straight man's. None of the friends spend time exclusively with the straight man's family.

In about a third of the friendships (n = 4), both men spend time with each other's families, either at their own homes or their families' homes. All the straight men and most of the gay men do not want the straight man's family members (except for their wives) to know about the gay man's sexuality. To this end, both men put an "I don't care what they ask, don't tell" policy into effect. The gay man does not express any homosexual behaviors or preferences that would reveal his sexual identity. And the straight man does not say anything that would reveal his friend's sexual identity. Often the two men go to extremes to keep the secret. For example, Grant, a gay man, asked Don, his straight friend, not to tell Don's parents that Grant was going to Washington, DC for the weekend. Grant worried they would figure out he was gay because he was making repeated trips to a "gay" city.

Two other friends, Mitch and Mark, who lived together, ran into many problems keeping Mark's parents and siblings from finding out about Mitch's sexuality. Mitch did not want Mark to have his son at the house because he did not want to influence the son in any way and he did not want anyone saying he did so later. Mark would not let any of his family members come to the house because he was afraid that they would think he was a bad person for associating with a gay man. Worse, if word got out it might travel to Mark's ex-brother-in-law, who would use the information to prevent him from seeing his child.

Because they keep their families in the dark about the uniqueness of their friendship, most of these friends avoid the family problems that the men who embrace their differences encounter. For example, they do not encounter problems with the straight men's family members disapproving of the gay men's sexuality or the straight men's friendships with them. They do not have to deal with either man's family thinking the straight man is gay because he has a gay friend. Because none of the friends spend time with the straight man's children, none of these friends have to negotiate how the gay man should act around the straight man's children. However, these straight men, like those who embrace their differences, revealed that they do not want their children to see homosexual behavior. So, if the two friends ever want to socialize with the straight man's children, they will have to address this issue.

The remaining friends, less than a third (n = 4), are brothers. Obviously these men have spent or do spend time with their families together. All of these gay men are out with the adult members of their families. But many of these family members do not accept the gay man's sexuality. Each straight man believes his gay brother should be the sole distributor of information about his sexual identity. To this end, they observe a "don't ask, don't tell" policy while with their families. The straight brother does not talk about his brother's personal life or sexual issues. When asked, he either answers honestly yet vaguely, or instructs the person to ask his brother.

EMOTIONAL COMMUNICATION

These friends are not as mutually intimate as those who embrace their differences. The gay man's emotional intimacy in these friendships falls below that reported in studies of friendships between gay men. The straight man's emotional intimacy exceeds that reported in studies of friendships between heterosexual men. His comfort parallels the way most straight men find emotional intimacy with women easier than with straight male friends.

Expressing Emotions

In most of these friendships (n = 11), both men share their feelings and thoughts about the nonsexual aspects of their lives, such as other friends, family and financial concerns, career and school issues, and nonsexually related health concerns. However, according to both men, the straight man shares more. Although the straight man (n = 11) talks about more personal issues such as his love life, his hopes and anxieties for the future, and feelings of anger and remorse, only a few gay men will (n = 4).

For example, Ted, a straight man, talks with Jeremy about his failures at work and the possibility of quitting and caring for his children full-time. Ted also talks to Jeremy about his disillusions with his church and religion. Cory described the problems his straight friend experienced about having a gay father:

> Cory: He came to terms with some issues that were going on in his family. His parents are separated but not divorced. His father is gay. And I think that concerns him to a certain degree. I didn't know this until after the fact. I knew him for three years and didn't know the situation. I think that he came to terms with that in that his father is gay and his parents are separating and that they don't seem to want to have a resolution to the matter. He was trying to have more of a relationship with his father. Although from what I understand now it is not so good.

The straight men said they find it easier to talk and share their feelings with their gay friends than with their other straight male friends. Many (n = 7) explained that they felt this way because by being out with the straight man, the gay man made himself vulnerable. To the straight man this meant that the gay man would not be acting "like a man," nor would he be expecting the straight man to act like "one of the guys." The "one-upmanship" (Tannen, 1990) dynamic of most men's friendships would be absent; he would not have to try to outdo his friend by being in control, unemotional, and on guard. He would not have to worry about being belittled or disregarded as he would with his other friends. Hence he could permit himself to be vulnerable.

The gay man in most friendships (n = 11) said he avoids topics that would acknowledge his sexual identity and would, thus, acknowledge the two friends' sexual differences. Most of the gay men do not discuss their troubles with family members or co-workers not accepting their sexual identity; or the frustrations they experience from daily reminders of their stigmatized and subordinated status; or how they think and feel about gay rights issues; or their thoughts and feelings about AIDS and HIV. When the gay men do talk about personal subjects it is usually a crisis. For example, Sal talked to Jake when the mother of his child denied him visitation with his daughter; Grant talked to Don when he had an identity crisis about being bisexual; and Cory talked to Tom when he left his partner of two years.

Most of the straight men (n = 10) feel relieved that the gay man does not share his thoughts and feelings about his personal issues. Listening to their friends reveal their inner selves would be too close to talking about homosexuality, which would make these straight men very uncomfortable. The straight man in five of these friendships, like those in cross-sex friendships (Buhrke and Fuqua, 1987), wishes his friend shared more with him. He wants to hear what his friend thinks and feels. He wants to hear about his friend's social life. He feels more comfortable and more accepting of his friend's sexuality than the other straight men who ignore their differences. He knows, however, that his friend distrusts him because he is straight. Even though this straight man acts more comfortable and accepting than most straight men, he is still a "man" and he may eventually act like a regular guy—homophobic. The gay man fears that if he truly was "just himself," as with his gay friends, his straight friend would feel anxious or disgusted.

Both the gay and the straight men described feeling anxious about expressing nurturing emotions for their friend, such as affection, admiration, compassion, and concern, as well as conflictual emotions, such as anger, disappointment, frustration, and annoyance. The straight man tends to be more anxious about expressing conflictual emotions than the gay man; the gay man tends to be more anxious about expressing nurturing emotions (n = 10).

The straight man gives his friend compliments. He tells him he is glad to see him, and that he cares about him. The gay man does not express such feelings for his friend because he fears his friend would question what it means when a gay man says "I care about you" or "I admire you." The gay man knows that even if the straight man did not interpret these expressions sexually, it might invoke an unwanted conversation about their sexual differences. Cory detailed the gay man's perspective:

> Cory: I think he is uncomfortable with me giving him compliments. I haven't really commented on the real personal things that I feel about him. But like I will say, "You look very nice," or "You're looking good these days," or "I like your hair cut; I like the color." He will say, "Well thank you." But I always feel like I can't become more personal because there have been times when I would actually like to tell him that I really care about him and I love him. I don't know if he would go too well with that. Even though he says he is comfortable with my sexuality and me being gay I still think that it would change the dynamics of our relationship if I were to be, I am not sure if it would freak him out. I think he would be very uncomfortable if he knew that I think of him so special. I am not sure how he would react if I said, "I think you are a very special person." For some reason I don't think he has had that in his life. I don't think there have been people that have been warm with him. I don't know if he would know how to react to that. Especially with a man.

Instead, the gay man described expressing these feelings covertly. By spending time with one another, calling and talking to his friend, and initiating coactivities, the gay man communicates that he likes the straight man and enjoys his friendship. In contrast, while the gay man expresses anger and annoyance verbally, the straight man only communicates his anger or annoyance covertly; by getting quiet or getting away from his friend. After his feelings subside, he acts as if nothing happened. For example, Don said nothing when Grant lectured him about drinking too much and destroying his life. He did not talk to Grant for several months afterward, though. Then he wrote him a couple of letters, asking how he was, with no mention of their argument. The straight man does not directly express his conflictual emotions for his friend. He does not want to hurt or anger his friend. As in most straight men's and most cross-sex friendships, these men do not discuss their problems.

Emotional Support

In all of these friendships, both men described doing emotion work for each other. For two reasons, though, the gay man usually does more (n = 12), just as women usually do more emotion work for men than men do for women. One, since the gay man often (n = 11) does not share his feelings and thoughts with his friend, the gay man does not give the straight man many opportunities to do emotion work for him.

A second reason is that the straight man in many cases (n = 10), like most straight men, lacks emotion work skills. The straight man will listen to his friend, but he does not initiate conversations about his friend's emotions. He does not challenge his friend or redirect his friend's emotions. He offers what he thinks is compassion, but it falls short of acknowledging the legitimacy of his friend's feelings. Instead, like many straight men, his way of being compassionate is often to offer a solution to the problem. Tom, reacting to his friend's distress about a recent breakup, reflected the straight men's style of emotional support:

> Tom: I just said, "Cory, think about it. If my girlfriend did this to me I would dump her in a second." I pointed out that if anyone else had done that besides his lover, say a friend or an acquaintance, he would not put up with it. I remember him telling me one time he was in some society or fraternity and someone came up and got in his business and was telling him what to do and he got right in their face and said, "This is my business; don't you worry about it." So he can handle other things fine. The night before he left [his boyfriend] he was really worried about going over there. I told him I have more confidence in him than in anyone else I know. He can put his mind to anything and get it done except when it comes to relationships.

In contrast, the gay man listens. He initiates conversations with his friend about his friend's life and feelings. He comments and tries to redirect his friend's feelings. If the straight man asks for advice the gay man gives it, but takes care not to hurt his friend while doing so. Jeremy explained, "I try to affirm him but not criticize him or hurt him." The gay man, though, realizes that his friend, in most cases, is not capable of returning this kind of emotional support. Jim explained:

> Jim: Steve lacked a strong male influence in his life. So for us being friends he's got a male bond. And I can see that. 'Cause we've talked about that. 'Cause he didn't have a very caring, nurturing father. He just wanted a man to hug him but not in a sexual way. Just to be hugged. A guy he can talk with and get some feedback. And it just turned out he can get that from a gay man and not a straight man because [of] those stereotypical behaviors—straight men can't hug, can't feel. But he could get it from a gay man as long as it was respected that this is not sexual. This is a hug, this is a friendship thing. And that was cool because that's all it was. But in turn I realize I can't get that back. He can't, I don't think he knows it, but he is not giving it back. I can hug him, but he can't hug me. And it is obvious that I need a hug. He needs the feeling but he can't return the feeling. And it might be the fear of him expressing something he is not ready to deal with yet.

Further paralleling cross-sex friendships, the straight man in these friendships described being more satisfied and closer with the gay man than with other male friends. Many of the straight men said they felt as if their gay friend was their brother. The gay man described being more satisfied with his other gay friends than with his straight friend. However, none of the gay men portrayed their emotion work as devalued, as women often do in friendships and romantic relationships with men. The straight men seem to genuinely appreciate and value their friend's emotional support. Many of the gay men said they feel good about helping their friends and about their friends trusting them.

SEXUAL CHALLENGES

As with those who embrace their differences, these friends experience problems due to their sexual differences. These friends have slightly different problems and issues, though. Neither the straight man nor the gay man in these friendships has trouble dealing with the gay man coming or being out. They do not have problems with heterosexism and homophobia from their family and friends, or from strangers and acquaintances. And, there is little erotic energy between them. However, these friends have major tensions due to the heterosexism and homophobia they bring to the friendship.

Coming Out

The straight man in almost half of the friendships (n = 7) knew his friend was gay when they became friends. He either knew from other people, or the gay man told him right away. The other half of the gay men came out to their straight friends after several years of friendship. They waited because they were not "out with themselves."[1] Once they were sure, they told their friends. These gay men were anxious about coming out, worried that their friends would reject them. None of the straight men reacted negatively to their friends' revelation. Most suspected their friends were gay all along, so it was not a shock. They understood that the gay men had to come out in their own time. Tom clarified:

> Tom: People told me he was gay before I moved in with him. And from the time that I met him when I was thirteen or fourteen I suspected he was 'cause if he talked about someone he would say, "There is this person I am interested in." He would never say a man or a woman. I knew. I felt bad that he couldn't confide in me that he was gay. I never, ever, said anything to him about it.

As with those who embrace their differences, the gay man in such a friendship said he had to officially come out to his friend, even if he thought his friend knew. He could not have a close friendship without being able to voice the words "I'm gay." The straight men agree, noting that they felt closer to their friends afterward, and became more personally and emotionally intimate with them. Steve elaborated:

> Steve: I think eventually it has to come out, that the sexuality issue has to come out. It was unspoken with us for a long time.

And we still don't talk about it often. But I think it was a big relief for Jim. And I know it was for me to just finally get it out in the open. 'Cause I don't know, maybe in the back of his mind, the whole time we were friends before I went over [to] his apartment that time he was wondering when I do tell him or when he does find out for sure is he gonna just drop me or whatever. I think you can only be so close when you have that issue or that boundary between you. Because he never knows whether I truly accept him as a friend for who he is. And vice versa.

Homophobia and Heterosexism

Unlike those who embrace their differences, these friends do not face homophobia and heterosexism from their friends and family members because they do not spend time together with them. And, since the gay man does not enact a gay identity, strangers do not suspect he is gay.[2] So, these friends do not face harassment from strangers and acquaintances when they go out together. However, both men hold prejudices that cause a great deal of tension and awkwardness between them. Both men, as described earlier, avoid talking about important life issues, joking around with each other, and sharing their feelings for each other.

Three quarters of the straight men (n = 10) revealed to me that they are at least mildly homophobic, that they hold heterosexist beliefs and values, and enact heterosexist behaviors. They show these leanings in three ways. One, the straight man said he would be uncomfortable if his gay friend expressed affection for his boyfriend in front of him. However, he will express mild verbal and physical affection in front of the gay man, such as hand holding or putting his arm around his wife or girlfriend. Two, the straight man dislikes his friend's gay friends because they are different from him. For example, Mike does not like or trust Todd's friends because they are effeminate. Lane, another straight man, expressed similar sentiments:

> Lane: It is kind of weird for me to go to those gay parties because of that. I don't feel like I have a lot in common with some of them. Unless I know them and I can talk to them. But

some others—I don't know them period. Or I may have heard of them but I don't know anything about them. And it is not like I can talk to them about girls or whatever. If I know they like to do stuff I like to do that is fine. But gay men tend to be—especially a lot of them that are effeminate—are not into things I like. They are into decorating and clothes. And that is not stuff I like to talk about.

Three, similarly, the straight man does not want his gay friend socializing with his straight friends. Tom added:

Tom: I'd invite him to my party but I don't know if I am comfortable with him being with my friends. And I am not comfortable with how they would be with him. I would invite him definitely but, you know, I'd understand if he didn't want to show up for some reason.

The straight men think they hide their homophobia and hetero-sexism from their gay friends. However, the gay men's accounts reveal that while they may not know the extent or the intensity of their friends' prejudice, they are aware of their friends' leanings. The straight man's behavior signifies that he does not like seeing or hearing about homosexual affection or attraction. He never asks the gay man about his date or partner, about what he did over the weekend, or about his hopes for marriage and children. The straight man's discomfort with seeing two men express affection shows in his avoidance of the gay man's partner or date and gay bars and parties. Though the straight man never voices his concern about the negative influence the gay man may have on his children, or his concern about what his family will think about him having a gay friend, he communicates these reservations by not inviting the gay man to socialize with his family.

The gay men are also homophobic. They show this in three ways. One, the gay men, not only the straight men, are uncomfortable with public displays of homosexual affection. They refrain from expressing affection for their partners while with their straight friends. One couple who live with the straight friend even go so far as to maintain separate bedrooms. Aaron is another good example. He is very close to his brother Matt, with whom he lives and owns a business. Unlike the other friends, they joke about sexuality. They talk specifically about Aaron's sexuality and the challenges it presents in his life. But, like the other friends, neither Aaron nor Matt feel comfortable with Aaron expressing affection for his date or partner in front of Matt. They legitimize this discomfort by arguing that public expressions of affection are not appropriate for anyone, gay or straight. It is more than that, however. Aaron acknowledged that his discomfort with his brother seeing homosexual affection comes between them. It prevents them from going to gay bars together, and it prevents Aaron from being himself with his dates when Matt is present. This is not a huge problem for him now because he is not dating anyone seriously. He perceives, however, that it will be a problem in the future.

Two, the gay man dislikes and distrusts his friend's straight friends because they are different from him. For example, Mitch dismisses his friend Mark's friends as rednecks and often teases them in front of Mark and teases Mark for being friends with them. Mitch's snobbery, described below, causes tension between the two friends.

> Mitch: I was very uncomfortable with the situation, thinking he was kind of from a redneck point of view and he has a wife and a little child. I was like I don't know if I want to get all involved in all this straight stuff because you know I am gay and I want to be that way. And I don't need the extra pressure. He would invite me to parties and things but I wouldn't go. I told him that people wouldn't understand my situation. And I did not want any confrontations and I did not want to have to beat anybody's butt. I just wouldn't go.

Three, as described throughout this chapter, the gay man in most of these friendships ($n = 11$), like most gay men, does not fully trust straight men, even this man. The gay man has learned, through repeated, daily rejection and discrimination, that most people, particularly straight men, do not respect homosexuality. Several of the gay men ($n = 6$) revealed that, given this social environment, it is hard for *them* to respect their sexuality. The gay men in all fifteen friendships have internalized, to some extent, the antihomosexual attitudes, values, and beliefs that surround them (Meyer, 1995).[3] The gay man thinks he is too different from straight men to be close to them. He does not think a straight man can be nonhomophobic. So, he keeps some space between himself and his friend, either by not being himself when with his friend, by not sharing himself or his life with his friend, or by distancing himself from the straight man's life.

The gay men in these friendships induce a self-fulfilling prophecy. By expecting straight men to act heterosexist, the gay men sustain low standards for straight men. And, with low expectations, straight men are not challenged to improve their behavior.

Eroticism

Compared to those who embrace their differences, these are not erotically dynamic friendships. Most of the straight men (n = 14) and none of the gay men share details about their sex life. Both figure that it would not interest their friends, that their friends would not relate to it. Or, they do not talk about their sex life because they do not want to hear about their friends'. While they do not discuss details, most of the friends do talk about homosexuality. The straight man sees the gay man as an expert who can confidentially answer all the questions about homosexuality that he was afraid to ask anyone else. These conversations run like question and answer sessions, in which the straight man asks questions such as, "How do you meet people? How do you know you are gay? When did you know?" These conversations are factual rather than erotic.

The gay man in a few cases (n = 3) worries that his friend worries that he will make a sexual advance. He worries that the straight man will misperceive his words or actions. Trent, who lives with his friend, commented:

> Trent: I think, there is, I mean in our relationship, there is always a sexual overtone. 'Cause I think all male relationships have those sexual overtones; they are just never addressed. But in our relationship they have to be addressed so that he feels comfortable in the fact that I am not looking at his butt every time he gets undressed, so that he feels comfortable sitting around in his underwear. Those kind of things have to be addressed.

None of the straight men, however, said they worry about their friends making sexual advances toward them. As recounted by both men, none of the friends ever had a sexual experience together. One set of friends acknowledged both to me and to each other that they wished they could find a man and a woman, respectively, with their friend's personality. One gay man, Grant, admitted that at the beginning of the friendship he felt sexually attracted to his straight friend, but did not act on it. Another gay man, Cory, worries that his friend wants something other than friendship from him. At times Cory and two other gay men, Jim and Mitch, have questioned their friends' sexuality. One of the straight men is married, one is divorced with a son, and the other has a girlfriend. These gay men base their suspicions on their friends' questions about homosexuality and their relative openness and comfort with sexual diversity compared to other straight men. Cory and Jim, two gay men, reflected:

Cory: And other things like wanting to experiment with anal sex, that he would actually like it if it wasn't for the stigma of being gay. I guess he is just open minded to that. He says, "Well obviously there is some pleasure involved." I don't think the average straight guy would admit that. That they are curious about that as straight men. They want to with women. But to say that, I don't think a lot of men would admit that or even think that. So maybe, he is just really comfortable with his sexuality. Sometimes I think he is really scared and then other times I think he is just really cool.

———————

Jim: It is the timing they choose to talk about it. And what questions they choose to ask. It is like if they are very intuitive questions, well-thought-out questions, it's not just on a whim they thought about it. And the moment they choose to ask can be when you are having a drink, when you are both alone, or at work. The other day Steve and I were alone in a room sitting and it was like his timing and he took a lot of time to ask his questions. So it is like so what is he asking and why? And it was very inappropriate for the timing but we were alone and that was probably the only time that he knew we would be alone and nobody would come in [and] interrupt me answering or him being afraid to ask the question. It was a definitely sexual question. And it was like he was just curious. He said,

"What does it feel like? How do you know what to do?" One of those kind of questions. And I was like okay, why is he asking? We've never had a very intimate kind of conversation before.

These gay men's suspicions illustrate how gay men add to heterosexism and homophobia. They do not think straight men can really be comfortable with sexual diversity and talk about it candidly. The sexuality of straight men who do is automatically suspect. These gay men are not raising their expectations of straight men, and they are not rewarding straight men for being nonhomophobic. Instead they dismiss the sincerity of these straight men. On the other hand, as I discussed in the previous chapter, and as Jim points out, many seemingly straight men use gay men. Hence, the gay men's suspicions are understandable.

CONCLUSION

These men's discomfort with their sexual differences keeps them apart. They try to deal with their discomfort by ignoring their sexual differences. They say they do this because sexuality is not, and should not be important to their friendship. In their eyes, they are beyond having to talk about having different sexual identities or having to show their sexual preferences when with each other.

In working so hard to make sexuality a nonissue in the friendship, they, ironically, make sexuality a central, albeit obscure, issue in the friendship. These friends neutralize the gay man's sexual identity, denying the importance of sexuality in his life but not in the straight man's life. They deem only the latter as applicable to their friendship. Because these men stifle that one part of the gay man, they are not able to build mutually close and significant friendships. Subsequently, these friendships are more important to the straight men than to the gay men. They are more emotionally intimate with the gay men than the gay men are with the straight men. For many of the straight men this is the closest male friendship in their lives. In contrast, the gay men are closer to and more emotionally intimate with another gay man. The gay men like their straight friends but they do not trust them.

Chapter 5

Struggling with Differences

This chapter includes the friendships (n = 16) in which one or both of the men do not accept or respect their friends' sexual identity. These gay men are not as comfortable with their friends as those gay men who embrace or ignore their differences. Like most gay, these gay men do not trust straight men. Similarly, most of these straight men resemble most straight men in that they are much more homophobic than the straight men who embrace or ignore their differences. These friends rarely have to confront their differences, though, because they do not spend much time together and are not emotionally or personally intimate with one another.

About two-thirds of these friends have always been casual friends. Like most gay and straight male friends, their discomfort with their sexual differences keeps them from becoming close friends.[1] To these men, the friendship is not important in their lives. The other third used to be close friends but the friendship changed when the gay man came out or came on to the straight man. These friendships are important to both men, and they are struggling to save them.

TIME TOGETHER

These friends are not nearly as close or as comfortable with each other as those who embrace or ignore their differences. They are casual friends. They know each other from work, school, or from living in the same neighborhood. They get together, usually to go to dinner or to a party or out to a bar, a couple of times a year. Their lives are very different. The straight man does not have time for the gay man. He is settling down, engaging in family-oriented activities with his girlfriend or family. The gay man in many of these friendships (n = 10) does not have time for the straight man either. He mostly socializes with gay people in the gay community, going to gay bars and keeping late hours. Neither friend invites the other to join him, and each would most likely decline the invitation if he did. Like most gay and straight male friends, the two men do not share similar interests and do not spend much time together.

As one straight man, Talbert, noted, both men feel as if they are on "the outside looking in" on the friend's life. Kamil, another straight man, added:

> Kamil: But because of Kris's lifestyle he is always on the go. He goes out every night. And coming home at three in the morning. It just doesn't allow you a lot of time together. I don't think we will ever be like we were. Things have changed too much. We will never be as close as we were. Just because society will never allow us to be. It is too hard for Kris. It is too hard for me. He's got to stand on one side of the fence and I've got to stand on the other. And you are always going to have that fence between you. Until society changes, until society learns to accept everybody's own private feelings we will never be as close as we were. In this time of age, the gay lifestyle and even the gay word in itself is not accepted. They are very much ridiculed and they are very much put down as weak. There is just not as many open-minded people. There is a lot more than you would probably think. But there is just not enough open-minded people to accept the gay society. And because of that they are outcast in a sense, they are confined to their gay bars and their gay bowling league on their only gay night, and that is why we are never going to be as close. 'Cause they don't have free reign. They don't have free roam. They cannot go down the street and hold their lover's hand like I can go and hold Anne's. It is not accepted. So he can't do it around me because I am a part of this society.

According to both men, they are not comfortable with each other. Their sexual differences make them nervous. While they are together, the gay man is on guard, and the straight man does not know how to act. The gay man thinks the straight man would not like him if he was totally out with him. The gay man thinks hearing about or seeing homosexual behavior would make the straight man very uncomfortable. Subsequently, like the gay men who ignore their differences, these gay men do not show homosexual affection or talk about sexual details with their friends.

However, unlike the gay men who ignore their differences, the gay man will not hide his sexual preferences in conversation. He will refer to himself as a gay man, refer to his partner, mention attending a gay bar or gay community events, use gay language and gay mannerisms, and casually joke about his sexuality. He is careful, though, not to say anything offensive, unlike the gay men who embrace their differences. As Dietrich stated, "I don't go out of my way to provoke anything by making comments. If it comes naturally, okay." The gay men will not act ultrafeminine, with feminine body movements (i.e., flaming) in front of their friends, though many do so when not with their friends (n = 8). Those who refrain from flaming say they do so because flaming is about politicizing sexuality, which they think is inappropriate with a straight man who is at least trying to accept them.[2] Rich, a gay man, commented:

> Rich: The whole purpose of flaming is just to blow these people's minds. I have a problem with that. There is a time and place for everything. There is a time to flame and there is a time not to flame. You learn how as a gay person not to be threatening toward straight people.

The straight men are aware of their behavior. Kamil noted, "It wasn't just something that I could accept. It wasn't something that I could just relax around." Many (n = 13) try to appear masculine when with their gay friends, just as straight men often do with their straight male friends. Talbert, a straight man, elaborated:

> Talbert: I don't know if I did this before, but I go out of my way to show my masculinity. I go that extra mile. But then again that may have always been me and I just didn't realize it. I am more self-conscious about myself around Bo. I am talking a lot more about sports. I talk about women more than I do my wife around Bo, women in general. I go out to eat with a

bunch of guys on Wednesdays and we see a lot of girls come in there and I caught myself, the last time I was over there talking to Bo that came out. And I was thinking, "Talbert, where did that come from? Why did you say that? What difference does it make what girls you saw today?" I am second guessing what I am saying.

The straight man also worries that having a gay friend will make him seem less of a man to others. The straight man can deal with his discomfort as long as the gay man does not show his "girlie actions," as Raymond put it, which call the straight man's identity into further question.

None of the straight men are sure how to act around their friends. There are no rules, no social norms to guide them. Most just try to avoid talking about anything personal, particularly anything having to do with sexuality. Talbert explained:

> Talbert: I don't know how to act around Bo now. I mean I treat Bo the same but his sexuality doesn't come out in conversations. I guess I am afraid—I don't know—I guess it just goes with me being uncomfortable with what Bo told me. Just because we were friends so long before he came out of the closet, before he even thought about this. But he never really, he told me when he figured it out and that's about it. And the way that he explained the way that he found out that he was gay. Those things really stick out in my mind. And with that in mind, my conversation with him has changed. I mean we still joke, we still laugh, we still have a good time, we talk about everybody else. But as far as his relationships or my relationships go, I don't know if he feels this way, but I know I go out of my way not to mention them. Once in a while I get ballsy and ask him, ask him if he is in any relationship or anything like that. For the most part, I try to steer clear of that.

EMBEDDEDNESS

These men embed their friendships in their lives much less than the friends who embrace or ignore their differences. Fewer socialize with their partners, family, and friends. Those who do, do so less frequently.

Partners

Many of these friends do not socialize with either man's partner or dates (n = 8). Some only spend time together with the straight man's partner (n = 5). Only a few spend time with the gay man's partner (n = 3), and then the straight man's partner is always with them too. Both men are more uncomfortable when with the gay man's boyfriend than are those who embrace or ignore their differences. Talbert described his difficulties:

> Talbert: The last time I went over [to] his house his partner was there and I had to ask him if that was his partner. He would not tell me. We stepped out back and I asked him. The partner was inside. I asked him, "Who [are you] seeing?" And he said, "Well, I am seeing Sven, the guy inside." It made my skin crawl a bit. When he said it then it didn't really bother me but when I came back in and I started noticing differences in body language that did make me uncomfortable. Eye contact, hand on knee, that kind of thing.

Friends

Several of the friends (n = 5) share a mutual female friend, the straight man's girlfriend, but otherwise most do not have mutual friends (n = 14). Most (n = 10) do not socialize with each other's friends either. Subsequently, they do not run into the problems of the friends who embrace or ignore their differences. They do not have to address whether and how to acknowledge the gay man's identity with the straight man's friends and family. The straight man's friends have no opportunities to harass the gay man, and the gay man's friends have no opportunities to hit on the straight man.

Most (n = 12) do not socialize with each other's friends because the straight man is uncomfortable doing so. Talbert is a good example. He does not want his gay friend to socialize with his straight friends because he thinks his straight friends might find Bo's lifestyle offensive. He worries that they might question his values and principles for having a gay friend. Talbert confided, "Well, it is very selfish, but I would be afraid of the way they would look at me." Similarly, Raymond, another straight man, worries that his straight friends might say, "Oh, I didn't know you had friends like that."

Likewise the straight man thinks that his gay friend might find his behavior with his straight male friends offensive. For example, Talbert makes sexist and heterosexist jokes and comments when with his straight friends. He would not be able to do that if Bo was with him, which would cause his straight friends to wonder why he was not acting like himself. The gay man knows that his friend worries about what his other friends will think about him for having a gay friend. But, as Bo conveyed, the gay man does not realize how much it bothers the straight man:

> Bo: Talbert has a really good friend who sounded like a traditional truck-driving guy. And I don't know if Talbert mentioned to him that the guy in Talbert's wedding was gay or something like that. But I don't know if he would feel comfortable. And he might have a little insecurity like gosh, this guy is going to think I am weird for having a gay friend. But I don't think he would let that worry him too much. He is just too secure. I mean what has he got to lose. It is not like he is in high school or anything and he has to be in the cool crowd or something. He has got a great wife, a happy life. So I don't think he would be embarrassed.

These friends rarely socialize with the gay man's friends because the straight man does not know how to act around them. He is uncomfortable with them. Again, he does not know what the rules are, what the norms are. What should he say or not say? What will offend his friend's friends and what will not? Talbert explained that in most cases he would rather not know the sexuality of Bo's friends because then he "would feel freer to talk openly about some subjects and not necessarily sexual preference subjects."

Family

Most of the friends (n = 13) never or rarely socialize with the straight man's family, particularly the straight man's parents and siblings. None of the friends socialize with the gay man's family. The straight man does not want these family members to know that he has a gay friend. When the two friends are with them, the straight man tells his friend not to let any one know that he is gay. He fears his family will think he is gay or denounce him for having a gay friend. Bud, a gay man, and Talbert, a straight man, recounted:

> Bud: I have been over to Clay's mother's house. She is definitely a gay hater. She didn't know. Clay told me what her views were because she is a real radical Christian. I didn't bring it up. I wasn't going to say, "Well, let's talk about it." She didn't say anything. He told me not to mention it. It would be whole lot of hassle to hear all this humdrum.

> Talbert: I got flack the first time with Bo. Dad and Mom went into this little lecture about birds of a feather flock together. So my friendship with him is guilt by association. I don't want their views of Bo to change. And I know that they would. They are very. . . . Dad is a Southern Baptist minister. Very conservative. Very, very hard headed about this. I mean it took him awhile before Dad could deal with a divorced couple much less this.

The straight man in these friendships, like those who embrace and ignore their differences, does not want his kids to see any homosexual affection. He trusts his friend will act appropriately around children. Raymond recalled inviting his gay friend and his gay friend's partner to a party:

> Raymond: They know that—from parties in the past—they know that when they come they act like themselves but they don't hug and smooch on each other around other people. But I would invite them. Like we invited them to our little girl's birthday party one year. They came. Both of them came over. Just as nice as they could be. Talked to all the other guests. They never smooched on each other. Never embarrassed anybody in front of nobody. They were just real good.

EMOTIONAL COMMUNICATION

These friends are much less emotionally intimate than the friends who embrace or ignore their differences. Emotionally, they closely resemble heterosexual men's friendships. Both men suppress their own emotional experiences when with each other and do not provide much emotional support to one another. They share less intimacy than most heterosexual female friends, most cross-sex friends, and most gay male friends.

According to both men, most of the friends were never emotionally intimate (n = 12). The gay man, like most gay men, revealed that he is afraid to share his feelings and thoughts about his life because he does not trust straight men. In addition, he worries that hearing about a gay man's personal issues might make the straight man more uncomfortable than he already is. The gay man does not share how he feels about his friend. He fears the straight man might misinterpret his expression as a sexual advance. Similarly, like most traditional men, the straight man shuns emotional intimacy with other men. He will share gender-appropriate thoughts and feelings with his wife or girlfriend, but not anything that would diminish his masculinity. He does not share how he feels about his gay friend for fear it might lead him on or hurt him.

Unlike those who embrace or ignore their differences, these friends do not even express affection covertly, as most straight men do. However, they do express their anger covertly, by not talking to each other for short periods of time. As in most heterosexual men's friendships, they do not discuss their conflict. For example, Bud's friend Clay got mad at him one night while they were at Clay's home, and he refused to drive Bud home. It took Bud three hours to walk home. He never said anything to Clay about it. Overall, these friends seem to be afraid that if they expressed their emotions for one another they would jeopardize their friendship.

Some of the friends (n = 4) shared emotional intimacy before the gay man came out or came on to the straight man. They shared their thoughts and feelings about themselves, their friends, and things going on in their lives. During these conversations they would provide each other emotional support; listening, offering advice and suggestions, providing compassion. Now neither man provides such support. The men's personal lives are now off limits.

For example, in the past, Talbert, who used to think of Bo as a brother, expressed all his feelings for Bo. He yelled at Bo and told him he was angry at him for driving drunk one night. He on several occasions told Bo he loved him. Since Bo came out, Talbert will not verbally express any of his feelings for Bo. He will not say he worries about him; that he thinks Bo is just going through a phase and needs more time to search his soul. Talbert will not tell Bo that he feels hurt because Bo told him last and that he feels angry with their mutual straight friends for trivializing Bo's new identity. Talbert will not tell Bo that he loves him and that he is afraid of losing their friendship. Talbert thinks Bo would abandon their friendship if he shared these feelings. He confessed, "I don't want to hurt him. That's the best way to say it. That's the reason I hide what I think. I am worried about how he views me."

SEXUAL CHALLENGES

As with those who embrace or ignore their differences, these friends experience many problems and issues due to their different sexualities. Unlike the other friendships, these gay men have a great deal of trouble coming out or being out with their friends. Both men bring their heterosexism and homophobia to the friendship, which keeps them from becoming closer friends. The most serious challenge they face is both men's anxieties about sexual advances and the gay man's sexual feelings for his friend.

Coming Out

These gay men are not out as much in their lives, or with their friends, as the gay men in the embracing or ignoring friendship groups. They are in the process of coming out. Many are not out at work or with all of their family members (n = 8). They lack the sexual confidence of the gay men who embrace their differences. But, unlike those who ignore their differences, they refuse to hide their sexuality.

All but one of the gay men enact a gay identity, or "act" gay. They talk with a lisp, use gay language, or talk nonchalantly about being gay or engaging in gay activities, and act effeminate. In many of the friendships (n = 10) the gay man is ultraeffeminate, adopting a feminine voice and feminine body movements. Many of gay men (n = 9) "look" gay; they wear clothes, jewelry, or their hair in stereotypically gay styles. None of these gay men are "straight" gay men.

Just over half the gay men (n = 9) explained that while they do not hide their sexual identity, unless someone asks, they do not announce it. None of these gay men ever verbally came out to their friends. They do not think it is necessary or appropriate. They think people can tell they are gay if they pay attention, as did the straight man in all these (n = 9) friendships. One gay man, Fabian, shared his thoughts on this strategy:

> Fabian: I am a firm believer in not broadcasting to the world. Now there are some who feel if they don't tell everybody and point their finger at them and say that "Hey this is the way it is with me and you have got to accept it" and most of the world doesn't accept it and they don't understand why they have created a problem. And I don't believe in that. I don't believe in hiding it. Say, if somebody asks you, it depends on why they ask you. . . . I still think it is a question that does not have to be asked. People these days know enough about what is going on in the world that they can figure it out. They don't have to ask you point blank.

In the past, straight men rejected several of these nine gay men after they came out (n = 4). Subsequently, these gay men are reluctant to come out to straight men now. Gabe depicted how a past rejection influences his current friendship:

> Gabe: I told Jackson in the letter that me and Rex were in love. I got a letter back from Jackson, typed, that said, "Dear Gabe, have a nice life. Jackson." And that was after sixteen years of friendship. And that really, really hurt. I was crushed. Totalled. That taught me a lesson to be very, very sure before you tell anyone.

The remaining gay men (n = 7) were not planning to come out to their friends, but either someone outed them, or they feared they

would be soon. Some of these gay men were not out with themselves for many years during the friendship. For some time, ranging
from one to six years, all of them (n = 7) knew they were gay and
pretended to be straight with their friends. These gay men suspected
their friends would not accept their sexuality and would reject the
friendship. As time passed, it became increasingly difficult for the
gay man to come out. He would have to admit to years of deception.
Though effective, carrying on this false persona exhausted the gay
man emotionally. Kamil elaborated:

> Kamil: Kris didn't want me to know, even have a clue, that he
> was gay. I didn't know. I had no idea. I didn't know until after
> I got out of school and that was last year. It hasn't been long. I
> have known Kris for six years. But I knew him for four years
> before I knew. I was the last person to know. Kris has always
> been feminine. And sometimes when we wrestled I would call
> him fag. But it was like a buddy thing. I did it to guys I played
> football with—call them faggot. But I had no idea that he was
> really.

Six years into his eight-year friendship with Talbert, Bo accepted
that he was gay. For almost a year Bo hid his identity from Talbert.
He lied when Talbert asked him what he did the previous night or
what he did on the weekend. He constantly worried that someone
would see him at a gay bar and tell Talbert. Finally Bo decided it was
time to stop hiding:

> Bo: One day I realized I was tired of lying to my close friends. I
> was drifting apart from them. I figured, you know, tell them the
> truth and you can either keep the friendship but don't let the
> friendship drift without at least giving them a chance. But with
> Talbert my main fear was that he was going to look at me and
> say, "You phony." I mean we were friends for I guess five to six
> years. We were really close friends. But, with Talbert more so I
> was afraid of him just saying, like pulling things out from my
> past, "You had that picture of Caroline on your wall back from
> when we were in the dorm and that was just to cover you up."
> "Well you have a picture of a Mercedes on your wall but you're
> never going to drive it, you know." That is one of my analogies

for describing why people stay in the closet for so long. You get social acceptance and that is what everybody wants out of life. So it was easy to stay. I thought I was happy with girls I was with. I was afraid Talbert would throw this one girlfriend in my face and be like, "You cried when you broke up with her. You said you were so in love with her." And I did. I thought I was. But now I realize that those feelings I am only really capable of having with a guy. Telling Talbert was really hard. I can't think of anyone who it has been harder to tell than him. Telling both of my sisters wasn't really hard. Telling him was hard. And I kind of feel bad. Not bad that I am gay but bad that I could have . . . that there would have been a better way. But you rehearse it for hours and when the time comes to sit down you just don't preface it. It is like, "Hey, guess what?"

After the gay man came out, the straight man expected him to become a different person and abandon their friendship. Talbert worried that Bo would immerse himself in a "gay lifestyle." He might only socialize with gay people; only go to gay bars, parties, or social events; only use gay vocabulary and mannerisms; wear gay hairstyles and clothes. Eventually, Bo would not be Bo. Bo explained, "He was really worried that I was going to like become like some big queen [a flaming gay man] that was trapped inside that was going to come busting out." Talbert saw little room for him in Bo's new life. However, only one gay man, Kris, changed in this way.

Heterosexism and Homophobia

Unlike those who embrace their differences, none of these friends spend much time together in public, so they have never had to confront a stranger's homophobia and heterosexism. However, the prejudices that both men bring to these friendships create a great deal of tension.

The straight man in most of these friendships (n = 10) holds heterosexist values and beliefs. These straight men not only acknowledge this, but some seem proud of it. It is part of who they are. In this respect, these straight men are much different from the straight men who embrace or ignore their differences. During our interview, these ten straight men revealed that they think homosexuality is disgusting and immoral. Several referred to their gay friend and gay people as "them." These straight men believe the stereotypes about gay men. They believe that all gay men are perverts; that gay men's main goal in life is to have sex, especially with straight men, and, subsequently, most of them will get AIDS. When they hear other people make negative comments about homosexual people they rarely say anything to stop them. Like most straight men, they worry about what straight people would think of them if they did. The straight men in these friendships will not go to gay bars or to gay parties or socialize with gay people in any public venue. They fear a straight person might see them and gossip about them. Marcus, a straight man, explained that he did not want to appear "hypocritical, to be saying one thing and doing another." These straight men (n = 10) think that gay men have a psychological or physiological problem and pity them.

How the straight men plan to raise their children illustrates their heterosexism. Several plan to use the friend as an example of wrong behavior. Talbert demonstrated:

> Talbert: I will let Bo come around the child. I am going to let my kid know about homosexuality. I am not going to let him find out from the streets. I am going to let him know. I am also going to let him know how I feel about it. In that respect I wouldn't mind Bo coming over here. My kid is going to know he is gay. But I also don't want my kid to have a . . . there is a fine line between drawing a prejudice against a gay person and accepting it as an acceptable lifestyle. And that is what I am going to have problems discussing with my kid. Because I want him to know that in my household it is not an acceptable lifestyle. But I don't want [him] to be prejudiced against those people either. It is going to be very difficult. But I think it can be done.

The gay men in these ten friendships realize their friends are heterosexist, but they still want to work on keeping the friendships, as Talbert's friend Bo illustrated:

> Bo: Talbert, since he's been with Tina, has gotten more into religion. They go to a Baptist church in town. Which is not necessarily bad, hopefully. I do feel like, on the negative side,

if I sat down with Talbert or Tina and tried to discuss deeply all of these feelings and all of these issues that we would get into a big fight. And disagree with a lot of stuff. But I think you just have to go for what you can get.

The gay man's homophobia, to some extent, limits all sixteen of these friendships. These gay men are afraid to be totally out. Most have not completely accepted their sexuality ($n = 13$). Like most gay men, they have learned that most people, particularly straight men, do not respect their sexual identity. And, unlike the straight men in the embracing and ignoring friendship groups, many of these straight men ($n = 10$) give their friend no reason to believe otherwise. If anything, they have reinforced the gay man's belief that most straight men are homophobic and heterosexist. Subsequently, these gay men keep an even wider space between themselves and their friends than the gay men who ignore their differences.

Why Friends?

Given that none of these friends are close, and many are homophobic or heterosexist, one wonders why they are friends at all. There are three reasons. One, in almost a third of the friendships ($n = 5$), the straight man is not heterosexist. He would like to be closer friends with the gay man, but the gay man's fear of straight men and his shame for his sexual identity prevent it. The gay man wants to be friends with the straight man because he wants to feel less different. He wants to be out and still fit in and be accepted. Cash and Theo, two gay men, clarified:

> Cash: He can do what I call "straight talk" and I can fit right in with him and talk with him. And it is not like he is talking about going out hunting or something and I don't know nothing about it. We can talk about numerous things. And have a conversation. And we just sit there and drink beer.

> Theo: I think it is really cool because I like hanging out with straight guys, and I am just starting to do that. It used to make

me feel kind of alienated that I didn't have any straight friends that were guys because I felt like I was real different. And it made me feel real. Even though mentally I felt, "Well, I am just as good as anybody else." I still felt like I was real different and that even though people didn't treat me any different, they didn't know. And they would treat me different if they knew and it would make me mad because I would be like, "Everybody loves me until they find out this one thing and that one thing matters."

Two, in another third of the friendships (n = 6) the men had formerly been very close friends, spending much time together, even living together, joking and talking about everything. Kamil, a straight man, noted, "He was like family to me. He was beyond a best friend." Half of the ten heterosexist straight men, discussed earlier, are in these friendships. Everything was fine until the gay man came out or came on to the straight man. Afterward, as Bo, a gay man, and Juan, a straight man in a different friendship, described, both the gay man and the straight man withdrew from the friendship:

> Bo: There was probably a couple of months where Talbert and I . . . when I first told Talbert we probably that first month talked on the phone three times. Whereas we used to talk on the phone three times a week. So it was strange. But I take 50 percent of that. Well, probably I take more than that because I hit him with something pretty heavy, not with something that is necessarily bad, but something that took a lot of processing. And maybe I should have helped him process but he didn't ask me to and I didn't want to overemphasize. I didn't want to call him and be rejected. I didn't want to call him and say, "Well, Talbert, you know I am gay and I know this must be hard for you; we can talk about it." And have him say, "You think you are that important." I didn't want to have that. So we just kind of shied away from each other.

> Juan: Then he fell in love with me. And it totally screwed our friendship up. And now we hardly even talk, which is bad

'cause I like him. It makes me feel now that the only reason why we were friends is 'cause he thought maybe he could turn me into his lover or something. Which makes me feel really bad. It really does. Because I respected him.

Three, in a third of the friendships (n = 5), the straight man harbors homoerotic feelings which he explores through this friendship. These men compose the other half of the heterosexist and homophobic straight men that I identified earlier. The gay man tolerates the straight man's heterosexism and homophobia because he knows that it is just a screen that his friend uses to hide or deny these feelings from himself and others.

Eroticism

Sexual tensions riddle these friendships, more than between the friends who embrace or ignore their differences. Each man worries about his friend making a sexual advance and each worries that his friend may misinterpret his actions as a sexual invitation. The friends who embrace and ignore their differences do not have these concerns. Jeremiah, a gay man, summed up both friends' concerns:

Jeremiah: You never know what anybody's intentions are. They don't know what your intentions are. They don't know if you want to get in their pants. And you don't know if they are being friends with you because they are just in the closet and won't come out. So both of you are sitting there going, "I wonder if I can say this, or that." That is why it is so much easier just not to assume or take anything for granted.

All the friends avoid complimenting one another for fear of sending the wrong message. Two friends, Cash and Raymond, provided more detail:

Cash: He is . . . well, he's a good friend—don't get me wrong. But he's the type I don't know how he would take something like that. So I don't necessarily make comments like that with straight people. I know some can handle it, no problem, but some will be like cut their eyes at you. So I really hold compliments to myself with straight men. I've told his girlfriend. I have complimented him to her. And she has kind of gotten it around to him. But direct, face-to-face, me and him, no I haven't made a comment.

Raymond: If I complimented them they may take it the wrong way. I just try to watch what I say. I will be friends with them but I try to watch what I say, 'cause I don't want him to take the wrong impression.

Many of the friends have reason to worry as several of the gay men are in love or in lust (n = 6) with the straight man. All these gay men have shared these feelings with their friends either verbally or by making a sexual advance. Several of these gay men (n = 4) became possessive of the straight man. The gay man feels angry when other gay men show attraction for his friend or simply talk to him. He feels jealous of the straight man's girlfriend. One gay man, Kris, even tried to break up his friend's romance. He spent time with each of them individually and criticized the other, and then prevented the couple from spending time alone.

The gay man's feelings for his friend cause him a great deal of heartache. Unlike those who embrace their differences and learn to incorporate their erotic feelings into the friendship, these gay men distance themselves from their friends. Likewise, the other gay men (n = 10) said that if they ever did become attracted to their friends they would end the friendship. It is simply too difficult. Rich commented, "It is like hitting your head against a wall." Marvin, another gay man, shared his experience:

Marvin: Oh, I mean I was awful in high school. I mean it was almost like I stalked him, you know what I am saying? I didn't think I was going to make it [a] couple of times because I was having to deal with the fact that I am a homosexual and that I liked a straight guy. But it was really hard. All through high school. My senior year was when I really started becoming hateful toward him because I knew I was leaving, and so I knew I had to deal with him and me being gone so I started becoming really hateful. Oh, gosh. We didn't have one nice thing to say about each other because I was pretty mad all the time and he would always say, "Why are you doing this?" And I would say that it was just my problem.

Surprisingly the gay man's feelings and actions caused the straight man in these six friendships little disappointment or anger. Only one, Juan, felt hurt by his friend's feelings for him. His concern for his friend, though, overshadowed his distress:

Juan: Well, he told me that he was in love with me. And he broke down and cried several times. He said, "I am just so overwhelmed and I just can't stand it." But at the same time I realized the pain that he must have felt being in love with someone that didn't love him back, who just wanted to be friends. But I was always straight up with him. I never led him on. I said, "Marcus, I will do anything for you. You don't have to do a thing for me. Just be my friend. Just give me your friendship. That's all I want. I will always be your friend." And if Marcus and I started talking I would be his friend again. But that one hurts. But I respect him enough to give him time to get over it so maybe we can continue our friendship some time in the future. I mean I want it. 'Cause he is very special.

The rest of the straight men in these six friendships dismissed the gay man's feelings and actions, immediately forgiving him. For example, Cash reported that after he told his friend he had made a pass at him the night before, his friend said, "What's done is done. Don't worry about it." Another gay man, Dietrich, hit on his straight friend Dylan repeatedly, even putting his hands in Dylan's pants and putting his arms around him. Dylan laughed it off:

Dylan: So then he starts feeling my shorts and he sticks his hand up my pants. And I am going, "Dietrich, bad boy, Dietrich. You shouldn't be doing that. You know my girlfriend wouldn't like that." And he said, "Oh, it just feels good; you don't mind it do you?" And I go, "Well, actually I'd rather you weren't doing it." Then he took his hand away. It was fine. It didn't bother me. I didn't feel humiliated or violated like a lot of people do. I don't know. You know I watched the *Howard Stern Show* once, and I thought: That guy thinks like me. Nothing fazes him. It really didn't faze me. I took the situation and just made it into a fun, humorous situation. I started running around to the other side of the couch. He would come over here and I would go over there saying, "I don't know Dietrich; I don't know about this." It just didn't really faze me.

As Dylan's excerpt suggests, some of these straight men seem a little too forgiving. They are playing along with the gay man's sexual advances. I suspect that these straight men are some of the "not-so-straight" men that the gay men in this and other studies report. In five of the sixteen friendships, both men provided information further supporting this possibility. Kris revealed that before Kamil had a girlfriend, Kris and Kamil shared sexual intimacy in many ways:

Kris: See, before they started dating he was with me every night. Not sexually. He would sleep with me and we would cuddle. And he'd be affectionate. I guess that is the reason I am mad. We will still be naked in front of each other, whatever. We don't care. We will go to the bathroom together. If we got to go, we got to go. He has told me before that if he was ever to do anything that it would be with me.

Another straight man, Raymond, who has three gay friends, seems a little too worried about being hit on. During our interview he revealed that his wife is the only thing keeping him from having homosexual sex. He also admitted he would like to hear about his gay friend's sex life. He said, "It would be really interesting how they do things. Just to listen to the different things they would do." Raymond summed up his concerns about gay men hitting on him:

Raymond: Then he wanted to know if I would have a relationship and I said, "No. It stops right here. I don't mind being friends with you but I will not have a relationship with you. I am married. I got kids. And I respect my wife. And I would never run out on her." Now I know AIDS is out. That is one reason why I don't get involved with gay people, which I don't want to anyway, but that is another reason too. But they tell me, "I want to go to bed with you and all that." I don't know. I know who the person is, but I don't know who they've been to bed with, you don't know what they got, this and that. And if I did go to bed with them what in the hell would I wind up with? What kind of disease? And then I would be carrying it home to my wife. She could get it. And I love my wife too damn much to be bringing that home.

CONCLUSION

Both men's homoerotic feelings and behavior and both men's homophobia and heterosexism cause the greatest problems in these friendships. It keeps the two men from being comfortable with themselves and each other, which keeps them from being close friends. All these friends are struggling to be friends. They want to be friends, but just cannot get past their different sexual identities. Their discomfort about having a friend with a different sexual preference overwhelms them and their friendship. They do little together and have trouble talking about everything, not just sexuality issues. They do not share in each other's lives. Many of these men want to have a closer friendship, but opening up scares the gay men, and the straight men either morally object to homosexuality or fear their homoerotic feelings.

Chapter 6

Power, Difference, and Multiplicity

I will now explain what we can learn from the three types of friendships described in the previous chapters. What motivates and enables them to be friends? Why do some friends accept and respect their sexual differences and others do not? Why are some closer, more emotionally intimate, and more trusting than others? The answer to these questions lies with the differences between the men's gender identities and the resulting balance of power in the three types of friendships. After presenting this argument, I will consider additional explanations. I end by discussing the implications of my analysis for integrating the sociology of sexuality and gender.

GENDER ENACTMENT

The way the men in each group enact gender influences their friendships differently. Table 6.1 summarizes these distinctions. The men who embrace their sexual differences value and enact behaviors associated with men and women. Neither man is stereotypically gay or straight, nor do they perceive each other as such. The men who ignore their sexual differences enact contemporary masculinities. Although neither is stereotypical, both men perceive each other as such. The men who struggle with their sexual differences enact vastly different gender identities. The straight men value and enact traditional masculinity. The gay men value and enact traditional femininity. Both men are stereotypical, and both perceive each other as such.

Embracing Differences

None of these men (n=13 pairs) believe stereotypes about gay men or straight men. None of them think being a gay man means being ultrafeminine, obnoxious, or perverted. None of them think

TABLE 6.1. Gender Enactment and Friendship Dynamics

	Embrace Differences (n = 13)	Ignore Differences (n = 15)	Struggle with Differences (n = 16)
Similar Gender Enactment	Yes, SM and GM Masculine and Feminine	Yes, SM and GM Masculine	No, GM Feminine and SM Traditional Masculine
Perceive Each Other Stereotypically	No	Yes	Yes
Spending Time Together Frequency What They Do Together Friends and Family Emotional Intimacy	Often Unconstrained Yes Yes—Both	Often Conditional SM's Partner and Mutual Friends No—Both	Rarely Limited No Yes—Both
Emotional Intimacy	Verbally and Physically Expressive and Supportive	SM Verbally Expressive GM Verbally Supportive Little Physical Comfort	SM and GM Inexpressive
Sexual Challenges	H&H Among F&F Eroticism between GM and SM	SM and GM's Heterosexism	SM and GM's H&H
Power Dynamics	SM and GM See and Treat Each Other as Equals	SM and GM See and Treat SM as Dominant	SM Sees Self as Dominant, Demands Deference GM Sees Self as Equal, Demands Acceptance

SM = Straight Man; GM = Gay Man; H&H = Homophobia and Heterosexism; F&F = Friends and Family being a straight man means being in control, insensitive, competitive, unemotional, or abusive of others. None of them think homosexuality is a psychological or biological disorder, or immoral. All of these men are both effeminate and masculine, and act this way in most relationships, both with women and with men.

They value and enact masculine behaviors in many ways. They do car and home repair together. They go fishing, camping, and to football games together. They express conflictual emotions for each other. And, perhaps most revealing, most of them still claim the identity "man." They described having a man's need and desire for sex, holding their liquor, and protecting themselves and their friends from physical harm. For example, describing how his friend's friend harassed him for being gay, one gay man stated, "I may be gay but I am still a man, and I will fight whoever gives me any shit." In another example, one evening while at the gay bar, two of the gay men I interviewed were drinking shots of cinnamon schnapps. One man said he would have to do it in two drinks because it was so strong. The other man said, "A man could drink the whole shot." To which the other man responded, "No, a man just doesn't throw up."

They value and enact feminine behaviors in many ways. They exchange gifts. They decorate their homes and go shopping for clothes together. They care for each other when they are ill. They borrow each other's clothes. They share their thoughts, emotions, and lives with each other. Both men provide and receive emotional support from one another. They express nurturing emotions for their friends. Besides telling their friends how much they appreciate them, these men show how much they care for each other by sending "thinking of you" notes; taking dinner over to the friend; or giving him a hug.

Ironically, letting go of the hegemonic goal of proving themselves to other men provides these men with a sense of security and efficacy, the very goals that hegemonic masculinity promises. Because of their egalitarian values and beliefs about gender and sexuality, these men are able to be close, even best friends, with a man with a different sexual preference, which most men would find threatening. All the men are also close friends with other men and women. They see themselves as being different from most gay and straight men. They seem relieved, perhaps even proud, because of this. They definitely like who they are. Being egalitarian and open-minded seems to be a source of self-esteem for them.

In many ways these men intentionally oppose and resist the gender order. These friends have moved beyond the heterosexism and homophobia that divide most gay and straight men (Lehne, 1989; Herek, 1987). But, they cannot completely avoid the heterosexism and homophobia in the world around them. They experience resistance and pressure to act like more conventional straight and gay men from their partners, family, and friends. All of these men at times confront these tensions and pressures, at times ignore them and at times give in to them. Further, there is a point at which these men experience internal pressure to conform to more conventional ideals about gender and sexuality. Two examples illustrate this.

First, many of them are selective in who they stand up to. None of the straight men related inviting their friends to social events with their co-workers, and only one gay man reported confronting his employer about heterosexist behaviors or policies. The people they confront tend to be people who have little power in their lives and who cannot cause them significant problems, such as brothers-in-law, neighbors, and casual friends. Second, the straight men in these friendships want their children to be straight and are raising them to be so. Neither the gay man nor the straight man wants these children to see homosexual affection.

So here we see that even these exceptional men hold onto some heterosexist values and, in doing so, they contribute to the maintenance of compulsory heterosexuality and hegemonic masculinity (Rubin, 1993; Cockburn, 1991). Like other social structures, the ideals of hegemonic masculinity cloud these men's thoughts, values, and preferences, keeping them from seeing all of their actions critically (Morgan and Schwalbe, 1990; Kohn, 1989). These men are moving in an egalitarian direction, however. If change is to occur, people with privilege have to be a part of it, and these men are a part of it, both their successes and their failures.

Ignoring Differences

Most of the men in this group (n = 15 pairs) enact a contemporary or a "new man" style of masculinity (Donaldson, 1993; Clatterbaugh, 1990) in this friendship and with other people. They try not to act macho or effeminate. They try to appear reserved and in control, but also attentive, caring, and sensitive. They still devalue feminine behaviors, though, and want to maintain their male privileges and power. This is a "softer, more sensitive style of masculinity" but one that nevertheless sustains the gender order (Messner, 1993). These friends are cautious in what they will do together, avoiding anything that calls attention to their gender or sexual identities. They do not joke about sexuality. They do not attend events in the gay community. They do mostly gender-neutral activities together such as going to movies and out to restaurants.

One man epitomizes the straight men in these friendships. He thinks it is fine for people, both men and women, to express their emotions; to cry if they are sad, to tell others how they feel. But he feels uncomfortable doing so. He worries about how people would perceive him and if they would think he is feminine. He avoids buying pastel color clothes, and would not be caught dead in a pink shirt. He thinks of his friend "as a human being, not as a gay man." On the surface this sounds admirable, but upon closer inspection it reveals that while he accepts his friend's sexuality, he does not respect it. Unlike those who embrace their differences, these straight men see homosexuality as a psychological or biological problem. It is something over which gay men possess little control. The straight men feel sorry for their friend's plight in life and commend him for his strength and perseverance. Because of this condition, the straight men think most gay men are very feminine, perverted, and obnoxious. Each thinks his friend is an exception to this rule, which is why he can be friends with him.

With one exception, none of the gay men in these friendships "look" gay (Chauncey, 1994; Weinberg, 1978). They are ordinary-looking men. They do not wear jewelry, or dress or groom themselves like male fashion models. Only a few are effeminate in their personalities, and that is not obvious without talking to them. None, not even the one exception, "act" gay (Bornstein, 1994; Callender and Kochems, 1985). They do not speak with a lisp, use gay language, or talk nonchalantly about being gay or doing gay activities. They are "very straight" gay men (Connell, 1992).

Although he may not be flaming, the gay man is still gay, and as such the straight man thinks his friend is more like a woman than he is. This belief allows the straight man to feel dominant with the gay man. Subsequently, these straight men feel no need to prove them-selves to their gay friends, just as many straight men feel liberated from gender expectations when they are with women (Lewis, 1978). With their straight male friends, they, like most straight men, only discuss information that is gender consistent (Snell, 1989; Bleiszner and Adams, 1992). Most straight men usually turn to a female partner or friend to discuss personal issues and vulnerable feelings about themselves or others (Weiss, 1990; Halper, 1988; Gaelick, Bodenhausen, and Wyer, 1985; Buhrke and Fuqua, 1987). The straight men in these friendships can be emotionally intimate with their gay friends without jeopardizing their gender identity. Still, the straight men worry whether their emotional intimacy with a gay man makes them less of a man, less heterosexual. One straight man admitted, "Sometimes I feel like as a heterosexual man it should bother me a little bit."

Similarly, while the gay men accept their friends, they do not respect them as straight men. Most straight men devalue and harass gay men, and act tough and insensitive with most people. A specific gay friend is an exception. As many gay men told me, the straight man is "not your average straight man," which is why they can be friends. He is still a straight man, though, and as such, he may eventually act like an average straight man. Hence, these gay men, unlike those who embrace their differences, distrust their straight friends. Because their friend is straight, they see him as more pow-erful and valuable than they are. They like having a straight friend. It makes them feel special. They have something rare—a straight man's friendship. Subsequently, they are more forgiving and toler-ant of their straight friend than they are of their gay friends. Antici-pating the straight man's reservations and fearing his rejection, they keep a safe interpersonal distance from him. They let the straight man set the terms of the friendship, do not talk about their sexuality, and repress their own emotional expression.

Somewhat reluctantly the men in these friendships simultaneous-ly sustain and resist hegemonic beliefs and values about gender and sexuality. The straight men are beginning to question the value of hegemonic masculinity but they still devalue femininity and homo-sexuality. Like the straight friends in Bird's (1996) study, they have eased off gender expectations with women and with nonhegemonic men such as this gay friend, but they have not made the leap to other men. In contrast, the gay men take a firmer grasp of gender expectations in these friendships, reinforcing the connection between masculinity, heterosexuality, and power (Morgan, 1992; Connell, 1987, 1992).

Struggling with Differences

In these friendships (n = 16 pairs) both men perceive each other stereotypically and both behave stereotypically. The straight men embody traditional, hegemonic masculinity, both with their friends and with everyone in their lives. They devalue femininity and homosexuality and can not tolerate "flamers" or "girlie actions." They are not emotionally expressive or nurturing with anyone, and trust few people.

Like those who ignore their differences, these straight men disapprove of homosexuality. But they go a step further. They think it is either a morally wrong choice, or a choice that one makes because of a psychological disorder. If they did not object to homosexuality and find it obscene, they think they would be less manly. They cannot see their friends for anything other than their sexuality. They think the gay man's sexuality rules his life. They worry that the gay man will make sexual advances. They worry that being associated with gays draws their masculinity and sexuality into question. Subsequently, to assert their identity to themselves and to their friends, they intentionally talk about sports and women and refuse to talk about their friends' homosexuality. They refuse to touch their friends; no hugs, no pats on the back, no handshakes.

The gay men embody everything the straight men devalue. They are very effeminate. They express their femininity and sexuality by using gay language and gay mannerisms, and often do so obnoxiously. In other words, many of the gay men are flamers. They tone down their sexuality and femininity when with their straight friends, but unlike the gay men who ignore their differences, they do not hide it. Many of the gay men are still constructing their own sexual identity. They are not completely comfortable with their sexual desires. They feel uncomfortable around straight men, afraid of feeling attracted to them or that straight men will only see them and treat them as sexual beings.

The straight men see themselves as more powerful and demand their gay friends' deference. In contrast, the gay men demand acceptance. Both men think the best way to protect themselves and maintain face in the friendship is to manage their own and their friends' emotions (Seidler, 1992; Brod, 1987). As found in research on relations between men, by expressing conflictual emotions and withholding nurturing emotions, the straight men try to (1) bolster their own masculinity, (2) induce fear or shame in their friends, and (3) make their friends feel insecure, invaluable, and subordinate (Clark, 1990; Messner, 1993; Tannen, 1990). Meanwhile, the gay men try to suppress emotions that might make their friends feel superior to them. By being emotionally inexpressive and in control, the straight men try to assert dominance and the gay men try to avert it. In doing so, they continue the devaluation of emotions and anything associated with emotions (Cockburn, 1991; Seidler, 1991a), perpetuating the social psychological basis of sexism and heterosexism (Kimmel, 1992; Herek, 1987).

As described in the previous chapter, given that the straight man in many of these friendships is homophobic or heterosexist, one wonders why these men are friends at all. In many cases the gay man tolerates the straight man because having a straight male friend helps him to feel less different, that he is less of an outcast. The men in many of the other friendships were close friends until the gay man came out or came on to the straight man.

On a positive note, as a result of these friendships both men are becoming aware of the gender order and how their beliefs, values, and behaviors sustain or resist it. The straight men believe in the naturalness of the gender order, and the legitimacy of their power and privilege. They intentionally sustain hegemonic masculinity and the gender order in these friendships. The gay men are beginning to question the legitimacy of the gender order. By expressing their homosexuality with their friends they resist this order, though not intentionally, and challenge their friends' beliefs, values, and behaviors.

Reproduction of Inequality

As the men in these friendships show, patriarchy, hegemonic masculinity, and compulsory heterosexuality are "deep structures"

(Sewall, 1992) that shape men's vision, beliefs, and preferences in their relationships with other men, as well as the social customs and laws they draw on to guide their actions in those relationships, and the social, political, and economic institutions in which those relationships occur. All the friends both intentionally and unintentionally oppose, resist, and sustain the gender order with each other (Connell, 1987).

Most of the gay and straight men in this study, like the nonhegemonic straight men in Bird's (1996) study, maintain that hegemonic rules are not a part of their identities. Yet they, at times, knowingly act hegemonically. They feel pressure to conform from their partners, family and friends, from strangers, and on the job. They often carry out hegemonic norms to avoid losing status, or being "pecked" by other straight men. Many of them, such as the men in Bird's study, relegate their nonhegemonic beliefs, values, and behaviors to interactions with women and nonhegemonic men. In doing so they sustain the gender order.

Others chip away at the gender order by expressing their nonhegemonic beliefs, values, and behaviors with each other and with other men. However, in that they are still men and many are white, they retain a higher social status in the eyes of others. We preserve these privileges and power in our laws, customs, and our ways of attaining social position (Segal, 1993). This provides them a kind of safety net. They have the luxury of being exceptional, of defying norms, with minimal negative consequences for their individual lives.

TAKING THE ROLE OF "DIFFERENT" OTHER

If my argument is correct, that the men's gender identities explain why some friends respect and accept their sexual differences more than others, then the penultimate question becomes: How did they develop those gender identities? Why are some of the men less hegemonic than others?

Although obviously a multitude of experiences went into this process, I found that one experience most of the men who embrace or ignore differences share is a past relationship with a "different" significant other. This person was a family member or a friend with a different skin color, a physical or mental handicap, or widely different religious beliefs. Many of the men had "different" friends because they grew up on racially and ethnically diverse military bases. Through this relationship these men learned to take the role of "different" other and to value doing so (Mead, 1934). They saw the world through different eyes. They experienced different ways of being and knowing. In many cases, they learned what it is like to be discriminated against because of some irrelevant characteristic. As a result of these friendships, they either overcame or never developed a fear of difference. They became tolerant of different people and willing to be friends with them.

Taking the role of different other shaped the way these men think, their meanings, beliefs, and values. Not all the men came to equally value difference though. Some, those who ignore their differences, moved beyond tolerance into acceptance of difference. And some, those who embrace their differences, went further and came to respect difference. These men, the least hegemonic in this study, experienced the most significant "difference" relationships, leading them to construct open-minded, nonprejudiced, nonjudgmental identities. These men made it a personal goal to accept and respect others. Many even chose careers that allowed them to nurture or welcome differences such as teaching, nursing, therapy, and art.

The men who are currently struggling with their differences, who are the least accepting and respecting, are just now, with this friendship, taking the role of different other. It is possible that with time these friends will parallel those who came to ignore or even embrace differences. In fact, as described in Chapter 3, many of the friends who now embrace their differences went through a difficult period in the past, early in their friendship, during which one or both men struggled with their sexual differences. These friends worked through these tensions, and in doing so, their friendship changed the man that each man became. Maybe those who are struggling with their differences now will do the same.

To more securely make this argument about the positive influence of taking the role of other, I would need to know how common the goal of accepting others and the experience of taking the role of a different other is among men in general. It would also be helpful to know what influence, if any, taking the role of different other has on the lives of men without cross-sexual friends. Although I do not know these answers, I do know that a clear pattern exists among the men I studied. By extension, if more people learned to take the role of different others and to value doing so, then they too might construct more egalitarian identities.

This finding has serious implications for social programs that promote interaction between different people, such as school deseg-regation and busing programs and cultural diversity programs in communities and schools. My study supports the theory behind these programs—interaction with different people increases toler-ance and acceptance.

However, as these men illustrate, one can take the role of other only so far. Two aspects of the gay man's life separate him from his straight friend; AIDS (Dowsett, 1993; Fish and Rye, 1991; Shilts, 1987) and living with a "spoiled" identity (Goffman, 1963; Warner, 1993; Sedgwick, 1990). Most gay men fear, suffer, and mourn the destruction caused by AIDS and HIV (American Medical Associa-tion, 1996). Their devalued sexual preferences ensure daily doses of discrimination, degradation, and rejection (Odets, 1995; Cochran and Mays, 1994). These experiences insulate gay men from straight men and bond them to other gay men and lesbians (Nardi and Sherrod, 1994; Nardi, 1992b; Kurdek and Schmitt, 1987).[1] Josh and Ted, two gay men, elaborated:

> Josh: I have a bond with them whether I am friends with them or not because we have all been through and go through some of the same B.S. So there is an automatic bond there no matter what. Like because I am black there is a bond there 'cause we still go through the same B.S. and that has happened a few times. So even though they may not be my friend, we just have a very strong bond because of our lifestyle.

> Ted: My gay friendships are a little closer. . . . also right now with death and everything it herds you in a corner. It is like if you were in an age group where people were dying you would be closer to those people. And . . . before that [before AIDS] there was still a camaraderie and that sort of thing. I am able to talk with my gay friends about relationships a little deeper.

And I feel a camaraderie, a closeness, or a protective feeling for my gay friends that I don't for my straight friends.

As Josh and Ted explained, the straight man can empathize but he has not experienced difference firsthand, as the gay man has. Consequently, the gay man in many of these friendships does not *feel* quite as close or as connected to his straight friend as he does to his gay friends.

ADDITIONAL EXPLANATIONS

Why are some friends more accepting and respecting of their sexual differences than others? I have argued that the answer to these questions has to do with the men's gender identities. In coming to this analysis, I also considered several alternative explanations from the friendship, sexuality, gender, and social psychology literatures. Below I review those that contribute to my explanation.

Gender on Reserve

In a 1994 study of straight men's friendships, Walker found that some of the men in her study were unusually close. She asked the same question I did—why? She ultimately concluded that class differences explain the findings for her study. She also considered that straight men with other sources of gender reinforcement, such as their appearance, jobs, marriage, or children, can afford to push gender norms. They reinforce their gender identities in other aspects of their life. Walker explained (1994:263), "They are not therefore faced with a problem of gender identity that they must reflect on and solve either through modifying their behaviors or through modifying their ideologies to better reflect behavior." This is a possible explanation for the straight men in my study. The straight men who embrace their differences, the least hegemonic and the most accepting and respectful in this study, are also the most attractive and physically fit by conventional standards. Their appearance may secure their masculine identity for them, alleviating their concern with doing gender hegemonically.

Sociodemographic Differences

The literature on men's friendships documents that friendship quality varies with sociodemographic characteristics such as length of friendship, friends' age, partner status, education, and class and race differences (Walker, 1994; Bleiszner and Adams, 1992; Allan, 1989; Franklin, 1992). I described these differences earlier in Chapter 2, and summarized them in Table 2.2. Except for those summarized below, no sociodemographic characteristics explain the differences in the friendships in this study.

The men who struggle with their differences have been friends for five to seven years less than the friends who ignore or embrace their differences, and they tend to be less educated. This could explain why they are less accepting of each other. Also, more men who embrace or ignore their differences have other friends with different sexual preferences, giving them more experience with the unique issues in these friendships. This may help explain why they have an easier time being friends than those who struggle with their differences. Compared to the men in the other friendship groups, among those who embrace their differences, fewer straight men have children and fewer gay men have partners. Combined, these characteristics may afford these men more time and energy for their friendship, enabling them to become closer friends.

Outness

Another possible explanation is that the timing when the gay man comes out to his friend influences the two men's comfort with their sexual differences. Many of the gay men in the closer friendships came out or were out with their friends early in the friendship. Both the gay and the straight man in these friendships said this brought them closer together, that the gay man's sexuality was a barrier between them until they addressed it openly. This explanation does not hold for those struggling with their differences, however. Some of these friends were close before the gay man came out. For them, the gay man's sexuality became a barrier when he verbally came out.

How out the gay men are in their lives partly explains the differences in the friendship groups. The more out a gay man is in his life, the more intimate and trusting he can be with others (Stanley and

Wolfe, 1980). The gay men who embrace their differences are the most out and the most close to their friends, followed by the gay men who ignore their differences, who are not as out or as close to their friends. The gay men who struggle with their differences are the least out and the least close to their friends. This explanation, though, misses part of the dynamic in these friendships—the straight friend. A gay man can be totally out and want to be close with his friend, but if the straight man fails to cooperate the two are not going to be close friends. It is necessary for the gay men to be out for the two men to be close friends, but not sufficient. The more out the gay man is the greater opportunity the two friends have to be close.

Furthermore, given that the gay man's level of outness influences how close the friends are, then the next question becomes: What influences how out a gay man is in his life? The answer, at least in part, refers to the one I offer—his beliefs and values about gender and sexuality. The more out a gay man is, the more personal self-exploration he has undergone (Tanfer, 1993; Odets, 1995; Ostrow and Wren, 1992; Cochran and Mays, 1994). It is difficult coming out and being out, especially in rural areas, where these men live. To get through this, they need to accept their gender identity and sexual desires, accept others', and accept that other people are going to object to theirs.

The gay men who embrace their differences have engaged in a great deal of identity work. They accept themselves and other people. The gay men who ignore their differences have done less identity work. They do not accept themselves or other's opinions of them as much as those who embrace their differences do. The gay men who struggle with their differences are still working through their gender and sexuality issues.

In-Group, Out-Group, and Reference Groups

Both the gay and the straight men in the embracing and ignoring friendship groups seem to get something from these friendships that they do not get from their same-sexual friendships with men. This friendship provides a space where these straight and gay men can be "offstage." With this friend they do not have to worry about fitting in or about being accepted, as they do with their same-sexual friends. This friend is not a part of either man's reference group. They do not evaluate themselves based on the reflected appraisals of this friend as they do with their same-sexual friends, who form their in-group (Shibutani, 1987).

The straight man in most of these friendships portrayed himself as more relaxed with his gay friend than with his straight male friends. He can just hang out and be himself with his gay friend. His gay friend offers him unconditional acceptance. The closeness these two friends share is often absent or awkward in most straight men's friendships (Reisman, 1990; Miller, 1983; for an exception to this pattern see Walker, 1994). As in cross-sex friendships (Snell, 1989; Buhrke and Fuqua, 1987; Williams, 1985) the straight man does not worry about being a "man" with his gay friend. He does not have to deal with his gay friend acting macho or expecting him to act macho, as he does with his straight male friends (Messner, 1992; Swain, 1989; Sherrod, 1987). He allows himself to do things with his gay friend that are outside the limits of most straight men's friendships (Nardi, 1992a; Hays, 1989). He reveals more of himself—his thoughts, emotions, concerns, hopes, and regrets. John illustrated:

> John: We relate to each other differently than straight males do, I think. It is not the butch, pat on the back, "Hey, let's go drink some beers." It is more in depth and honest with the conversation. And I tell him on the phone that I miss him or that I am sorry we couldn't get together this last weekend. Or I tell him that he is a wonderful guy. And that I'm glad he is my friend. Stuff like that. I can talk with him about more things than I can talk about with my straight friends. I feel more comfortable around gay men because I enjoy the openness in the friendship and stuff. 'Cause I think a lot of the ritualistic stuff—I've done it all—all the jock stuff, beating on each other, the first thing you do when you come over is pound the crap out of each other. But I think now I am getting older where I can appreciate other things.

Similarly, the gay man finds his friendship with the straight man refreshing because the straight man is not part of the community or the "family." The camaraderie that unites gay men also can stifle their friendships (Berger and Mallon, 1993; Nardi, 1992b). It is like living in a small town or being a part of a family where everyone knows everything about one another and judges one another accordingly. Ted clarified:

> Ted: I take everything in stride. You have to, being gay. It is like at the bar. Some people get upset, "They are talking about me." I say, "Well, I am sorry somebody is talking about you. If you walk into this bar you might as well be prepared. If you can't deal with that then you just need to stay home." That is what bothers me the most about people's attitudes in or out of the bar. They are so worried about what everybody is thinking or doing that they are not the same person they would normally be.

The gay man's straight friend does not know the gossip of the gay community. He does not criticize the gay man for his sexual politics as do the gay man's gay friends (Seidman, 1993; Rubin, 1993; D'Emilio, 1983). He does not comment on whether the gay man is too out or not out enough, too gay or not gay enough, or speculate on the consequences of his personal politics for the gay community. Some gay men share more of their thoughts and emotions with their straight friends because it is less risky. Trip added:

> Trip: John and Mavis are my closest friends here. I can tell them, I don't tell my gay friends everything like I do them. Because, I trust John and Mavis so much more than . . . I mean I trust Matt and Jeff but there is still that little gay thing going, where people . . . the gay family is so small here that everybody, eventually, even accidentally, knows what everybody else is up to. 'Cause there are too many people, and I don't think my friends are necessarily the kind of people that call people up and say, "Well, guess what he just told me." I think sometimes things come out accidentally, you mention them and it comes out.

As Trip described, like the straight men, in many ways the gay men can be "offstage" in this friendship too. They can relax and escape from some of the pressures of the gay community (Moon, 1995).

INTEGRATING SEXUALITY AND GENDER

My findings illustrate that our standard conceptualization of gender and sexuality, and our theories of the relationship between them, limit our understanding of men's behavior. Sociologists widely accept that patriarchy, hegemonic masculinity, and compulsory heterosexuality are linked; that we cannot be free of gender oppression while sexual oppression remains (Connell, 1993). Our concepts do not reflect this link.

As the friends in this study demonstrate, we can experience and construct potentially endless combinations of sexual and gender desires, behaviors, and identities (Laumann et al., 1994; Bem, 1995). Some gay men are masculine, some feminine, and some are androgynous. Many, at times, feel other-sex as well as other-gender desire. For example, a person can have an X and a Y chromosome and identify himself as a masculine woman who feels same-sex desire. He knows himself as a lesbian trapped in a male body. To others, this person would seem to be a straight man.

Our standard sexuality and gender concepts do not reflect this reality. To understand men's behavior more clearly, we need to integrate the sociologies of sexuality and gender. We can begin by moving away from dichotomies (Sedgwick, 1990).

Benefits of Integration

The benefits of moving away from dichotomies are widespread. I will highlight two. First, it would move concepts and theories away from destructive "us versus them" politics. Isolation fuels cultural subordination. Conceptualizing gender and sexual multiplicity might help people see that they share similarities with people they identify as different from them and differences with people they identify as similar to them. This understanding could encourage integration of various peoples and communities and transform contemporary sexual politics (Namaste, 1994). Working together, we can change local institutions and social environments more widely and more quickly.

Second, conceptualizing multiplicity would emphasize the political goal of "sexual liberation," which includes all people who oppose heterosexism and homophobia (Moon, 1995). Currently, we refer to "gay rights," which attracts only queer people who are out.

Abandoning an "us versus them" mentality would help move our efforts away from another political dead end—choosing or ranking one standpoint, be it race, class, gender, or sexuality, over another (Anderson and Collins, 1992; Collins, 1990). And, conceptualizing multiplicity would clarify our understanding of how dimensions of oppression and privilege intersect to shape life chances and experiences.

Advancements Toward Integration

Steps toward integrating the sociology of sexuality and the sociology of gender include a symposium of papers in *Sociological Theory* (Seidman, 1994) and *Theory and Society* (Connell, 1993) and articles addressing heterosexism in all the recent anthologies on men and masculinity and feminism (Connell, 1995; King, 1990). Recently, Bem (1995) argued that sociology would benefit from moving conceptually toward exploding or "turning up the volume" on gender categories rather than toward eliminating or "turning down the volume":

> I propose that rather than trying to dismantle the two-and-only-twoness of gender polarization and compulsory heterosexuality by *eliminating* gender categories, we instead dismantle that two-and-only-twoness by *exploding* or proliferating gender categories. In other words, I propose that we let a thousand categories of sex/gender/desire begin to bloom in any and all fluid and permeable configurations and, through that very proliferation, that we thereby undo (or, if you prefer, that we de-privilege or de-center or de-stabilize) the privileged status of the two-and-only two that are currently treated as normal and natural. (p. 330)

Despite their limitations, the friends in my study who embrace their sexual differences are an example of men moving away from a binary way of seeing and expressing sexuality and gender. These men express a multitude of values and behaviors together. They play, watch, and talk about sports together. They go fishing and wrestle with each other. They pat each other on the back, as well as massaging each other's back. They greet and part each other with a kiss and hug. They dance together. They go to family reunions, weddings, births, baptisms, gay bars, coming-out parties, and pride festivals together. They use gay language, joke about sexuality, talk about attraction to men and women, and talk about straight and gay sex. They show affection for one another by sending "thinking of you" notes. They value their own and their friends' emotions. They share their emotions about themselves and their lives, as well as their emotions, both nurturing and conflictual, for each other. They exchange emotional support.

If the above paragraph was about two women, it would not seem extraordinary. Women have been exploding and turning up the volume on gender and sexuality for a long time. Women have been able to construct femininities that include being independent, autonomous, assertive, caring, and sensitive. But, we consider this behavior for two men, particularly a gay and a straight man, avant-garde. While not yet there, these friends are moving toward valuing masculine and feminine behaviors equally, and heterosexual and homosexual desires equally. They are moving toward resisting or rejecting the power and privileges awarded or denied them because of their sex, gender, race, and sexuality. They show us that, as Bem suggests, one does not have to reject gender to reject these privileges. Instead, we can embrace gender.

Of course, these privileges will not disappear just because these men and others like them stop expressing masculinity in hegemonic ways. However, if more people do what the men in these friendships do, then we will stop associating behaviors and characteristics with one sex, and we may come to value them equally (Bem, 1976). Following this reasoning, by doing gender we could undo gender.

Bem's argument would work if masculinity, most notably hegemonic masculinity, did not center around domination and control. Men can reject their privileges and value behaviors associated with femininity, but as long as they continue to value the ability to dominate and control others they will use sexuality and gender as a means to do so. Getting men to stop valuing the ability to dominate and control requires more than, as Messner (1993:733) stated, "a shift in style of hegemonic masculinity." It requires "a shift in the social position of power."

CONCLUSION

The phrase "shifting the social position of power" may guide our future efforts to integrate the sociology of gender and the sociology of sexuality. Our theories of gender need to problematize and politicize heterosexuality. We need to illustrate how gender and sexuality simultaneously organize our social, political, and economic lives. Our concepts need to reflect that we can experience and construct potentially endless combinations of sexual and gender desires, behaviors, and identities. This work should make people aware, particularly white heterosexual men, of their heterosexism and how we reward them for it. Perhaps most importantly, we need to determine how to best encourage heterosexual men to value and execute sexual equality. Overall, to understand men's behavior, we need to see and explain the power of gender and sexuality, as well as the sexuality and gender of power, in men's lives.

Chapter 7

Methodological Reflections

In this chapter, I take a critical look back on this project, identifying issues to be addressed in future research. I begin by discussing the potential limitations of the sample, pointing out how these limitations may influence the analysis and conclusions I draw from these data. Next I describe the potential biases due to researcher/participant dynamics, including gender, race, class, and sexuality. I end by reviewing the impact of the study on the lives of the men I interviewed.

SAMPLE LIMITATIONS

My analysis and conclusions speak predominantly to friendships between white straight men and white gay men who are out, do not have AIDS and who are not macho. This study excludes gay men who are not out with their straight friends. My sample only includes a few gay men who are out with their straight male friends but not out with most other people in their lives. This sample includes only one friendship between black men, and only one friendship between a straight man and a macho gay man. Further, I was unable to clearly address friendships between gay men with AIDS and straight men.

On the surface, the apparent uniqueness of this sample would seem to seriously limit any conclusions drawn from it. However, the sample does not include many of these other types of friendships because there are few of them. My sample, analysis, and conclusions represent types of cross-sexual men's friendships that most frequently exist. I will now address each of the sample biases in more detail.

Gay Men Who Are Not Out

I restricted this study to friendships between out gay men and straight men. I did so because I wanted to focus on how the men deal with being different. If the gay man is not out, the two men do not deal with their sexual differences. Further, such friendships are rare. As the men in my sample show, it is too difficult to carry on a friendship in the closet. While doing my fieldwork I talked with a few gay men who had straight male friends with whom they were not out. For example, one black gay man told me of his closet friend of twenty years, a black straight man. The gay man was the best man in the straight man's wedding, is a godparent to both of his children, visits with his friend regularly, and often vacations with the straight man's family. The straight man does not know his best friend is gay. The gay man lives in fear that his friend will find out.

By networking in gay bars, support groups, and activist groups, I excluded most of the gay men in the town who may be out with their straight friends but not out in most other aspects of their lives. Gay men who are mostly in the closet do not go to these places. They cannot afford the risk of being seen with gay men. Excluding closeted gay men is an unavoidable problem in most studies on gay men (Tanfer, 1993). By definition, these men are nearly impossible to find. Even if you could find them, they would not talk about their sexuality because in doing so they would have to come out. From my fieldwork I know that there are very few of these types of friendships. Gay men who do not want to be out reveal their identity to few people. Otherwise, it gets tricky for them to manage who "knows" in a small town.

Macho Gay Men

My networking strategy also resulted in excluding macho gay men.[1] These are gay men who identify with and enact traditional masculinity.[2] (The men in the 1970s band the Village People are "ideal types.") I inquired about macho gay men during my fieldwork, and learned that macho gay men tend to isolate themselves from the gay and the straight community. They form their own small groups. There are few macho gay men in the community I studied. One night while at the gay bar I saw a man wearing leather and chains. I asked a gay man I knew to introduce me to him. He told me that most macho gay men are not friendly, especially toward women, and they tend not to be as out in their lives as other gay men. He doubted this man would talk to me and, not wanting to talk to him either, would not introduce me to him.

This gay man's analysis later made sense of my limited interactions with macho gay men. Through my community action work, I met a few macho gay men who were members of a masculine gay men's group. Unlike all the other gay men I spoke with and interacted with, these macho gay men were uncomfortable with me. They would not make eye contact with me or talk with me.

My analysis of my interview data includes one macho gay man. I gained access to him through my snowball sample. He has two straight male friends with whom he is out, his brother and a co-worker. We had a difficult time in the beginning of the interview. He would not talk. He kept getting up and sitting down, leaving the room, and wanting to talk about other things, such as his latest home renovation project. He eventually became more comfortable and talked for two hours. Afterward he mentioned that he had told me more than he had told his therapist. Since then, I have enjoyed numerous interactions with him and his partner during my activist work.

Given that macho gay men tend not to be out, I suspect that friendships between straight men and macho gay men are rare. None of the gay men I met during my fieldwork knew of any macho gay men who had a straight friend. I suspect friendships between straight men and macho gay men would have unique characteristics and challenges. These friends could have an easier time than the friends I studied since their gender and sexual differences would not constantly face them. My understanding, based on my fieldwork, is that macho gay men are not publicly affectionate with their partners. So these friends would not have to deal with tensions regarding seeing and expressing homosexual affection, which proved to be a major issue for the friends in this study. Further, these friends would have the advantage of similar gender identities, also a major issue in the friendships in this study. In this sense, friendships between straight men and macho gay men probably operate similarly to friendships between straight men.

However, for two reasons I doubt that these men are likely to be close friends. One, macho gay men, following characteristics of traditional masculinity (Clatterbaugh, 1990), are probably less attentive, less emotionally expressive, and less intimate with their male friends—gay or straight. Two, given that macho gay men are probably less publicly affectionate and less disclosive about their sexuality, they would likely conceal their personal lives, preventing the two friends from sharing their lives. In this respect, friendships between straight men and macho gay men may parallel those in this study who ignore their differences.

During this project, I met and talked with several men who are dating men in the military. According to their descriptions, these military gay men are macho. Since they spend a great deal of time with straight men, it is likely that these men have straight male friends. However, because of the military's "don't ask, don't tell" policy, these gay men probably are not out with their straight male friends. The gay men I spoke with thought a study on these friendships would be invaluable, but difficult to do because of the military's policy. If anyone found out about a serviceman's participation in the study he would be discharged and his career would be ruined.

Black Men

Cross-sexual friendships between gay and straight black men is another topic that I was unable to address with this study. These friendships are also rare, not just in the town I studied but across the United States (Peplau, Cochran, and Mays, 1997). Intense heterosexism and homophobia exist among black straight men, making it harder for black gay men to be out in black communities (Cochran and Mays, 1994).

I interviewed one pair of black friends and several black gay men who were friends with white men. In addition, I spoke with several black gay men during my fieldwork. All of these black men confirmed that few black gay men have black straight male friends, and those who do are rarely out with them. One evening while at the bar, one black gay man explained:

> Black straight men are even more hostile toward gay men than white straight men because black men are brought up to be

tough, macho kind of men who don't have any tolerance for wimpy men. Having been brought up like that, I don't let any of my black friends know I am gay. I learned to act the part of a black straight man—to dance, to know the music, the walk, the attitude. I think because of this I fit in better with straight people than gay people.

A study targeting cross-sexual friendships would be easy to do on the one hand, but nearly impossible on the other. Someone networked in the gay community could easily generate a snowball sample because, as I learned in my fieldwork, most black gay men form very strong, familial friendships with other black gay men.

However, because of the intense heterosexism in the black community and the likelihood that the gay men would not be out with their friends, studying both sides of the friendship would be difficult. Researchers would need to take extra efforts to protect the gay men's identities, and the gay men probably would not want their friends interviewed. They might grant access to him with the assurance they would not be outed. But, ethical concerns regarding informed consent and covert research activities would then rise.

Such a study, however, would provide insight on several issues unresolved in this study. First, it would provide a window on how gay men carry on friendships with straight men with whom they are not out. Hiding one's sexual identity for a prolonged period is extremely difficult. Even if it is possible to avoid being outed by others, it is very easy to slip oneself. For example, the one black man I met during my fieldwork who is not out with his friend of twenty years told me that his friend wanted to take him to a concert as a birthday gift. The straight man asked the black man who he wanted to see. The gay man, not thinking, responded, "Barbra Streisand." His friend said, "What?" Barbra Streisand was not the appropriate black straight male response. The gay man had slipped and given his honest reaction. They went to the concert, but the gay man could not enjoy himself. He worried that he would start singing or crying, as he usually does while listening to Barbra. Accordingly, a study on cross-sexual friendships between black men would highlight masculinity issues for gay and straight black men.

Gay Men with AIDS

I learned through my fieldwork and my activist work that friendships between gay men with AIDS and straight men are also quite rare. The gay men in four of the friendships in my analysis told me they have AIDS. It is likely that some of the other gay men are HIV positive or have AIDS and did not tell me. My sample includes a disproportionately high number of these friendships because I based it in a town where people with AIDS across a two-hour radius come, and often relocate, for treatment.

These friendships are rare because AIDS quarantines the gay community from the straight community throughout this country and most other industrialized countries (Dowsett, 1993; Shilts, 1987). Although the stigma associated with having AIDS or HIV is decreasing in the gay community, it remains prevalent in the straight community (American Medical Association, 1996; Sigelman et al., 1991). Hate crimes are increasing against gay people and people known to have AIDS or HIV (Comstock, 1991; Fish and Rye, 1991). Not surprisingly, most hate crimes are committed by straight men against gay men. Given these hostilities, gay men with AIDS or HIV depend almost exclusively on members of the gay community for the emotional, economic, and social resources they need to live. In doing so, they become even more isolated from the straight community.

The four friendships between gay men with HIV/AIDS and straight men in this study reflect these issues. There is a great deal of tension in these friendships. The gay men often shut their straight friends out of their lives when they are going through rough physical and emotional periods. During such times, these men want to surround themselves with people who understand their illness and who can help. Inexperienced with losing a friend to AIDS, the straight friend's emotional distress would only drain energy from the gay man. The straight men become frustrated during these periods, and find their friendship to be an emotional roller coaster.

I noticed that the straight men in all the friendships in which the gay man had AIDS or HIV were reluctant to talk about AIDS and HIV issues. These men knew I knew, but often simply stated that they still would not talk about it because they wanted to respect their friends' privacy. I think a project focusing on these friendships would need to ask questions specifically addressing the unique issues these friends face. Such a project would also need to take extra measures to ensure confidentiality and train interviewers to deal with intense emotional issues.

RESEARCHER/PARTICIPANT DYNAMICS

My status as a young, white, straight, educated, economically advantaged woman raises numerous methodological limitations in a study on men's emotions, gender, and sexuality (Kane and Macaulay, 1993; Williams and Heikes, 1993). Gender issues framed every interview, so I will focus on them and discuss the others along the way.

On the one hand, my gender, age, class, and sexuality may have inhibited the men's behavior and disclosure. The men may have only expressed or disclosed information they deemed appropriate for a young, white, privileged, straight woman to see or know. Depending on their sexuality, age, and economic status, they may have felt pressure to act appropriately with a woman of my status by signifying gender, using proper manners, and following social etiquette. Further, they may have expected me to act appropriately by looking and acting feminine, speaking correctly, or being embarrassed by what they said. They may have felt uncomfortable or threatened by me when I did not. Conversely, my gender and unthreatening persona may have enhanced the men's disclosure with me. They may have felt less pressure to maintain appearances, and shared more personal and sensitive information with me. This often occurs in studies involving female researchers and male participants (Morgan, 1992; Warren, 1988).

I started the research prepared for the men to find me inhibiting. I found that, with few exceptions, they did not. I expected sensitive issues to arise during the interviews, such as the men's sex lives, secrets between the two men, painful memories, and the sorrow and anger of the present (Tanfer, 1993; Coxon et al., 1993). I expected some of the men to hesitate before sharing their thoughts and emotions on these subjects. Some I thought might find the questions too personal. Others might question the confidentiality of our discussion. In either case, I thought they might worry about how their answers would make them appear both to me and to others. This, however, was not my experience. As described throughout the previous chapters, the men shared very sensitive and personal information with me. And they expressed a wide array of emotions. Many cried and laughed, showed anger, guilt and shame, and many expressed love and gratitude for their friend.

Exceptions: Race, Class, Sexuality, and Gender

There were times when, acting appropriately, several men treated me as a young, innocent, privileged, sheltered woman. Many gay and straight men apologized for swearing in front of me or using offensive language such as "pussy" or "bitch" or "dick." A few men hesitated before mentioning drug use, expecting it to shock me. After telling me the details of his sex life, one man stopped and sat silent for many seconds. Then he said, "I don't think I should say anything about that." I, thinking it was a confidentiality problem, turned off the tape recorder and began reassuring him of confidentiality. Then he said, "We were doing drugs." I attribute the men's expectations more to my youthful appearance than to my gender.

The gay men protected my personal safety on numerous occasions. As described earlier, for many months I went to the gay bar two or three nights a week. The bar is located in a section of town with a high crime rate. Consequently, many of the men were concerned about me entering and leaving the building safely. On weekdays the bartender allowed me to enter the bar before it officially opened, before crowds gathered outside. On weekends I arranged to meet one or two gay men at another location and then went to the bar with them. When I left, one or two men always escorted me to my car.

Several men also protected me at the bar. Two examples illustrate this. First, one night while talking casually with three gay men I had already interviewed, a black man approached, asking if any of us had jumper cables he could borrow. Everyone shook his head "no." He looked at me, and I, eager to return some goodwill to the gay community, responded joyfully "yes." Being a weekend night, when people pack the bar and the DJ plays louder music, none of the men around me heard my response, nor did they notice me leading the man outside.

I was at my car, pulling my cables out of the trunk, when the man asked, "Could you drive me to my car?" Responding "Okay," I was opening the car door for him when one of the men, a black man, whom I had been talking with in the bar, came outside. He asked, "What is going on?" He advised me not to offer my cables to this man or take him anywhere in my car. They started arguing. Another man I had been talking with, a white man, came outside and showed similar concern for my safety. The man needing cables accused the black man of being an Uncle Tom, protecting a white woman from a black man. Then a bartender, a white man, came outside. Soon all four men were discussing my safety and the merits of protecting oneself versus helping strangers.

By now I was scared. I had figured out that the three gay men I knew did not know this man, my assumption upon offering cables to him. I told the stranger, "I better not take you." The three gay men and I went back into the bar. They lectured and teased me for the remainder of the evening about naively putting myself in danger. One gay man later told me that a similar situation had occurred months before and that the person who offered assistance is now missing. Notices went out to everyone in the area alerting them not to offer assistance to strangers asking for cables. Since I was not going to the bar then, I did not get this warning.

On another evening, an older man in a tailored suit came into the bar. With the suit on, he caught my attention. I had never seen him before. I noticed him talking with one of the managers, and then he disappeared into the back of the bar. It was a rainy, cold, slow night and since I knew all five people in the bar, I went into the video game room to play Ms. Pac Man, determined to reach a high score. In a few minutes the man in the suit came back and leaned over the machine and watched me play. He was very close—inappropriately close. I was going to quit playing because I did not want to miss an opportunity to interview an older gay man. He said he enjoyed watching me play, and started putting quarters on the screen, offering to pay for additional games. From the corner of my eye I could see that his heavily starched white dress shirt was now open down to his belly button, exposing a black bra. We talked about the bar, how long it had been there, when it was open, and who went there. He then wanted to know who I was and what my sexual preference was. I told him about my study, which he was eager to participate in, even though he was only in town on business for that one evening.

Throughout this conversation I noticed that the bartender, whom I knew well by this time, kept coming back taking things out of a storage closet next to the video machine and then quickly returning them. I thought this was odd, but dismissed it. After three games my wrist was becoming tired, so I told him that was it for me. He begged me to keep playing. By now even I, Ms. Naiveté, figured out that this man would likely soon be "playing" alongside me. Upon returning to the bar area, the bartender and the other men immediately flooded me with questions and concerns. Not knowing the man, and spotting his black bra, they worried about me and monitored us the entire time.

Professional Distance

Fortunately for my study, I had interviewed all these gay men before they became "protectors." So these incidents did not bias the information they shared with me. However, my relationship with these gay men raised the likelihood that people would label me a "fag hag," which could negatively influence how prospective interviewees would see me (Moon, 1995).[3] A fag hag is a woman who socializes nearly exclusively with gay men. Fag hags are similar to female groupies. Members of the gay community assume fag hags are social failures. Subsequently, they often look down on fag hags.

I did not want to be known as a fag hag. I wanted and needed to be respected in the gay community to obtain valid, reliable information. I think my involvement with the community action organization, which had become widely known, prevented this label from being assigned to me. Only three gay men, all on the periphery of the community, treated me as a "fag hag" after I interviewed them. They called me several times a week, sometimes in the middle of the night, wanting to chat or asking me to go out to the bar. I did not accept these invitations, and maintained a professional distance from them.

Regarding professional distance, several of the men discussed severe emotional and psychological problems during our interviews. One gay man with AIDS revealed clinical depression, one gay man revealed an incestuous relationship with his mother, another gay man revealed childhood abuse, and several straight men revealed same-sex desires and questioned their sexuality.[4] Several men called me wanting to talk about these issues after our interview.

Others approached me when I saw them during my fieldwork. The seriousness of these issues caused me to question my obligations to these men. I decided I held an ethical and professional responsibility to suggest psychiatric consultation to them and, in the abuse cases, encourage it.[5]

Moreover, many men told heart-wrenching stories of rejection and personal anguish. Many men described great courage and virtue. Other men shared disturbingly callous and prejudiced attitudes, beliefs, and behaviors. I was able to distance myself emotionally from most of the men during the interviews, and maintain a dispassionate perspective on their accounts during my analysis. However, several of the men and the stories they told touched me profoundly, shaping our interaction during the interview and, later, my analysis of their accounts. These men illustrated complete acceptance and respect of themselves and others. Their self-awareness and self-security center their vision and their space in the world around them.

A few of these men are straight, and a few are gay. Four straight men amazed me. They described unusual egalitarian values and behaviors, empathy and caring for others, and nonjudgemental perspectives. These men understand their power and control in life begins and ends with them. They take responsibility for themselves and their actions. I felt equally amazed by the stories and lives of three gay men who saw the adversities in their life such as discrimination, harassment, and AIDS as personal challenges. Working to understand both their oppressors' hatred and their own fears, these men not only overcame these challenges but found inner peace, strength, and love. They have dedicated their lives to helping and teaching others.

These straight and gay men are exceptional, possessing wisdom and insight beyond their years. I was eager to learn from them. I believe these men recognized the sincerity of my enthusiasm and admiration. I could not hide it. Fortunately, they seemed appreciative of my emotional expression, which probably enhanced their disclosure and intimacy with me.

Later, my high opinion of these men tainted my early analyses and writings. I struggled with grouping friendships in which one man was exceptional and the other was not (n = 3). The exceptional man in these friendships seemed most similar to the men who embrace their differences. Because of the other man, though, the dynamics and issues between these friends mirrored those between friends who ignore or struggle with their differences. I went through several iterations of analyses before establishing a final grouping. I resisted critiquing these men and their friendships. I reworked my thinking and my writing many times. Eventually, I understood and explained these men as attainable role models, rather than mythical heroes.

IMPACT ON THE MEN'S LIVES

From what the men told me, participation in this study influenced them and their friendships positively, though not always tranquilly. Discussing their friendships made several men acknowledge problems and realize how much they value their friendships.

Revealing Problems

Our discussions often revealed problems to the friends. For example, one gay man described several times how his friend helped him over the years. He then went on to describe several times when he had not helped his friend when his friend had needed him. This man, showing visible guilt, started making excuses such as, "Oh, I had to work" and "I was dealing with my own problems." Another man, while discussing his disappointment with his friend over a recent conflict, realized that this was not an isolated incident and that his friend had been mistreating him consistently. His voice getting louder and his face becoming red, he became noticeably angry during this segment of our interview.

During the interview, many gay men and straight men recognized their own homophobia and heterosexism. For example, I always asked a straight man what he felt and thought about his friend holding hands with his date or partner while with the straight man. Following that discussion, I asked what he felt and thought about holding his wife's or girlfriend's hand while with the gay man. Many of the straight men who presented themselves as accepting confessed that they did not want to see their friends kiss or hold their partners' hand but they would not think twice about kissing or holding their own partners' hand while with their gay friends.

Similarly, I always asked a gay man whether he held his date or partner's hand while with his straight friends and while with his gay friends. Similarly, several of the gay men who stated that this friendship was no different from their other friendships went on to describe how it was different. They do act differently around their straight friends than around their gay friends. They do not talk about certain subjects, express homosexual affection, or use gay mannerisms or gay language when with their straight friends.

The contradiction between these gay and straight men's presentations of self and the accounts they offered often hit home for them. During these segments of the interviews, these gay and straight men showed shame by becoming quiet and looking away. Their voice dropping in tone and volume, they verbalized their shame by saying things such as, "Oh, I can't believe I just said that." Or, "I guess I have my own prejudices."

Other men acknowledged through their behavior that our interview exposed their heterosexism and homophobia to them. They became noticeably irritated with me for indirectly pointing out their prejudices. For example, Blake insisted that he acted the same with his gay and straight friends. But he told a story about not holding his date's hand while at his friend's wedding. When I asked if he held his date's hand at a party he recently threw, his demeanor changed from humorous to defensive and his body language changed from relaxed to upright. He looked me dead in the eye and responded, "Well I don't act, by asking that I know that you are not insinuating that I act in any way different." He then confessed that he did not hold his date's hand in front of his straight friend at that party.

Friendship Enrichment

As a result of our interviews, many of the men who ignore or struggle with their differences realized the importance of their friendships to them. These men pledged to work on their friendships, deal with their differences, and let their friends know how they felt about them. For example, during our interview, Cory said:

> It is funny that as I talk about Tom I realize that I really like him a lot more than I think I do. You are really making me think about how special he is to me.

During my interview with Tom, several weeks later, Tom showed me a card that Cory had just sent him. It read, "Thanks for being my friend." For two other friends, Jake and Sal, the interview brought their problem—the gay man's sexuality—out, literally. Before the interview, Sal never formally came out. Jake knew Sal was gay, and Sal knew Jake knew, but both were afraid to address it. Consequently, Sal repeatedly turned down Jake's invitations for Sal and his partner to join Jake and his wife for dinner. After my first interview with both friends, Sal and his partner went to dinner at Jake's house. Jake described the benefit of participating in this study:

> Jake: Sal said, "There is this woman who is doing this study and she was asking for other people's names that might assist her in gathering the data and I recommended you. She might be really interested in talking with you." I said, "Sure Sal, that sounds great." And he said, "Now I don't know if you know what is going on with this. It will be funny. You might know, you might not, I don't know. But we'll talk about it after." He has been laughing about it a little bit. I said, "So, you know I am going to go meet with Jammie today." He laughs and says, "We are going to get together and talk about this afterward. Don't talk about it with me in the office." I say, "All right, Sal, all right." So I don't know if this was like a mechanism. But it has always been unspoken. Like I understand, but there needs to be, I think, some naming of it. This will definitely give us a way to begin talking.

Many of the gay men who struggle with their differences hesitated for several weeks, even months, to put me in contact with their straight friends. These men were growing apart. The gay man worried that asking the straight man to be in this study would cause more problems in their troubled friendship. However, in several cases, the men told me that talking with each other about doing the interview broke the ice between them. By participating in this study they showed each other that they both cared about their friendship, that it was worth the struggle.

Chapter 8

Conclusion: Activism
As an Unintended Consequence
of Value-Committed Research

Through doing this research, I became a participating member of a community action group. This work adds great meaning to my life. I am helping to make a difference, to make social change. Most sociologists preach that, but few do it (hooks, 1984). Here I will discuss how I became involved with this social change organization, my role in it, and how I am applying sociological expertise to work toward social justice. First I describe how my identity as a community activist influenced this research.

INFLUENCE OF ACTIVISM ON RESEARCH

During the first five months of this project, I had trouble finding gay men who had straight friends. I gave presentations at all the support groups in town. Since most of the men who attend these meetings are not totally out, most do not have straight friends with whom they are out. I started going to the gay bar but gained few interviews. I got the impression that most people in the bar did not know what to make of me. I looked straight. I was not trusted.

I started doing second and third follow-up calls to men I had already interviewed, asking if they knew any more men I could interview. During one of these phone conversations, a gay man told me he wanted to start a community action group. He invited me to attend the first meeting. I went. I hoped it would be one way to get more interviews. It did. It opened up the entire gay community to me. The people at the first meeting were the inner circle of the gay community. Through my work with this organization I became very active and well known in the gay community. More important, I became respected and trusted. My interview rate skyrocketed, as did the intensity and frequency of my fieldwork.

My involvement with this organization granted me an insider's view on nearly all aspects of the gay community. It enhanced my understanding of gay men and the role that friendships play in their lives. Because of the severe stigmatization they experience, gay men's friendships are often their main source of emotional, social, and instrumental support (Meyer, 1995; Hays et al., 1990). This is why the gay community is so important to gay men. Their friends are their family (Nardi, 1992a; Weston, 1991). Gay men who lack friendships often experience emotional and physical problems, such as depression, anxiety, low self-esteem, and psychosomatic physical symptoms (Peplau, Cochran, and Mays, 1997; Berger and Mallon, 1993; Kurdek and Schmitt, 1987).

My involvement in this organization also enabled me to take the role of "different" other. I got to taste firsthand the daily discrimination gay men experience. My boss, upon hearing of my planned speech in a public forum, which was to receive wide media coverage, reminded me of my professional association with a medical school. He advised me not to say anything that would contradict the official medical doctrine on sexuality. Furious, I asserted that I would not be representing the university or the medical school, that I would be representing me. He apologized later, but the aftertaste remained. My boss never would have said anything to me if I intended to speak at an African-American festival or a conference on women's rights. Shortly thereafter the *Journal of the American Medical Association* published work from Gagnon's research team depathologizing homosexuality. I gave my boss a copy.

GETTING STARTED

At the first meeting, we decided to meet once a week to consider the issues involved in starting a community action group: organizing it, defining our goals and mission, identifying our geographical domain, and obtaining nonprofit status. We identified two key issues we would need to address: (1) whether to have a social change agenda; and (2) how to be inclusive, which in this community includes not only race, class, and gender but sexuality, level of outness, and health status. There are divisions in this gay community between gay men and lesbians, homosexuals and bisexuals, homosexuals and transgenderists, black queers and white queers, and to an increasingly lesser extent, queers with AIDS and queers without AIDS.

Perhaps the biggest division in the gay community is between those who are totally out and those who are not. The people at the first meeting estimated that at least half of the gay community would not want a group doing local political work and they would not attend any public social events. The risks that they will be seen by family, co-workers, and church members are too high for them. Not-so-out queers also worry that public events will push the envelope too far, making the local social environment more hostile. This tension over not pushing one's sexuality into other people's faces came up repeatedly in the gay community during my fieldwork, both in the support groups I attended and within the community action organization. Most people in this community think sexuality should be private. A few, including myself, think gays and lesbians should be able to express affection publicly as heterosexuals do.

At the first meeting we hashed these issues out for a couple of hours. Then I said, "We could do a survey to help us decide what the community wants and what they will support." They quickly nominated me to chair this committee and conduct a survey. In a few weeks we put a survey together and began administering it to people at bars, support groups, social events, and meetings across the 250 miles of our service area. At this point, my identity evolved from researcher to activist. I became a part of the "we."

Meanwhile, during our subsequent meetings we turned to other issues. We had to establish the structure of our organization and define our mission and goals. We decided our main goal would be to link gay people and communities across our region. We also decided to structure inclusivity into our organization by writing into the by-laws that there would always be two cochairs, one woman and one man. We debated many times whether to do something similar to ensure racial inclusivity. However, since there were so few black people in the group we worried that we would not be able to fill such positions, a requirement to maintain nonprofit status. I suggested that one of our main goals should be to develop heterosexual allies and increase acceptance of queer people in the straight community. I suggested that we target heterosexual people in positions of power, such as business owners, legislators, and church leaders. We eventually adopted this goal.

In three months, we administered our survey to over 100 queer people. I analyzed the data, looking at the similarities and differences in what people wanted across age, race, gender, economic, and sexual characteristics. The survey findings indicated that we needed to hold multiple events, address multiple issues, and keep participation costs down if we wanted to attract people of all ages, races, genders, and sexualities. Most people supported a peaceful, quiet social change agenda. No one wanted a march or a rally. Considering the survey findings, we decided that our major event would be a festival where we could have multiple activities to attract diverse people. The two main goals of the festival would be to bring the gay community together and to assert presence to the heterosexual community. Both of these goals became an issue of contention with the owner of the local gay bar. He voiced his opposition with several members of our organization. He did not want us attracting local attention to gay issues.

This man's opinion and actions concerned members of our organization. He was probably the most powerful person in the gay community. Without his support many members doubted we could work toward our goals, let alone meet them. We discussed his objections at length. I said that he was against the group for two reasons. One, he makes his living from queer people not having any other safe places to go. Two, he fears our activism will increase hostility in the local area, which could result in stricter laws regulating his business and in more hate crimes committed outside his business, driving up his costs. We decided to proceed without his consent.

We wanted to have free admission at the festival so we began fund-raising. We held dances, drag shows, pot lucks with key speakers, and music festivals. Besides raising over $7,000, these events and the survey also had the desired consequence of making people aware that there was now an organization planning events and working for gay acceptance. People were becoming excited. Members reported that countless people in bars, support groups, social events, and other meetings across the region expressed enthusiasm for our work. The bar owner, noticing this wave of support, agreed to hold a dance at the bar during the festival.

We held the first gay pride festival in this area in September 1995. It was a huge success. Over 300 people attended the main event, an outdoor fair on the town's largest public park. It consisted of educational, political, and spiritual speakers, tents with vendors and organizations from across the state, and entertainment such as dancers, musicians, and drag queens. I gave the closing remarks.

In December 1995, the members nominated and elected me to the board of directors. Since then, I have served as the chair of the board of directors and as president. I have helped coordinate numerous services, events, and fund-raisers. I promoted our work and our organization on the radio, television, and newspapers.

SHIFTING THE POSITION OF POWER

Over the last four years, we have worked to build and strengthen the gay community and to combat heterosexism and homophobia in the straight community. To this end, since our first year, we have held annual festivals, mobilized the gay vote, developed homophobia workshops, volunteered time in homeless shelters, and hosted workshops, conferences, picnics, town meetings, and Coming-Out Day celebrations, not to mention hosting numerous fund-raising events such as drag shows, formal dinners, dances, skate-a-thons, yard sales, and concerts. With all our programs, we strive for gender and racial representation by having diverse entertainers, speakers, and leaders at our events. As a result of our work, we have observed significant improvements in our local social and political climate.

Festivals

Since the first year, we have held annual festivals on public grounds. All have received widespread media coverage. Over 300 to 500 people have attended each festival. As with the first, the festivals consist of educational, political, and spiritual speakers, tents with vendors and organizations from across the state, and entertainment such as dancers and musicians. The festivals are preceded by musical or theater art productions and educational workshops and are followed by political rallies. The festivals have all been free and open to the public, ensuring that people of all walks of life can attend.

The festivals help build and strengthen the gay community. They are the only regular event in this area that brings lesbians, gay men, bisexuals, and transgenderists together in a public arena to assert a presence in the mainstream, heterosexual community. Without events such as this homophobia and heterosexism will continue to thrive. Gay people will continue to hide. In order to achieve sexual equality in this area people need to unite and demand their rights. This annual event is slowly helping to empower gay people to take these steps.

Homophobia Workshops and Community Volunteerism

We have developed a heterosexism and homophobia workshop that we have presented to all the city council members, the mayor, and administrators in the local department of human relations. We have offered to present this workshop at all the churches, businesses, and civic organizations in the region. We presented it in other cities across the state and at annual National Gay and Lesbian Task Force (NGLTF) meetings. We also determined that doing "good deeds" in the straight community would go a long way in combating heterosexism and homophobia. We named such deeds "community action." For our first event, we helped clean a local homeless shelter.

Mobilizing the Gay Vote

After the first festival, we turned our attention toward mobilizing the gay vote in local and state elections, and sensitizing politicians to that vote. Knowing that politicians often adopt an "all or nothing" stance on minority issues, we decided the most effective way to elect unprejudiced politicians was to unite with African-American groups in the region. Members of our organization began communicating with officials in the African-American organizations, predominantly church groups, across the region. Fortunately some of these leaders were open-minded and eager to work with us for social justice. We joined with them in marches and rallies against local racism. Then we asked for their assistance with the massive voter registration drive we were planning.

We invited politicians, business and church leaders, and civic groups to several workshops we held on organizing minority voter registration efforts across the region. We worked with local black churches and gay and lesbian organizations to register minorities across our region. We offered our assistance to the U.S. senatorial challenger, a black man. He accepted and campaigned here numerous times.

With the news spreading that we had registered nearly a thousand people across the region, we became a legitimate political force. Gay issues and the gay vote became attractive for the first time ever at the local level. In the next local election, the mayor spoke to the gay community for the first time at an event held by our organization. During that same election year, a black city councilwoman and the former mayor, a black man who ran for state senate, spoke at our festival. Furthermore, that year our U.S. congressional representative, a black woman, wrote a letter welcoming people to the festival.

Community Workshops, Conferences, and Picnics

The goals of the workshops, conferences, and picnics are to help (1) identify needs and (2) build, strengthen, and link gay communities across the region. The workshops are targeted to new lesbian, gay, bisexual, and transgenderist groups who need help getting started. The workshops focus on goal setting, organization building, networking, and fund-raising. The workshops have been conducted for audiences in towns across the region.

The conferences were held at a local university in collaboration with a student organization. The conferences brought together rural leaders and activists to network, exchange ideas, and learn ways that they and their organizations could be more effective in the work they do in their communities. Over sixty-five leaders from throughout our state and neighboring states attended the conferences.

Similar to the workshops, the community picnic is intended to help get a new rural organization on its feet or to reenergize an existing organization. We have offered to cohost picnics with several groups in neighboring rural towns. Besides food, a recent picnic featured performances by well-known musicians, educational information, and networking with community organizations. As a result of the picnic, the local community is stronger as is the tie between the cohosting organizations.

Coming-Out Day Celebrations and Town Meetings

We have hosted several events to celebrate national Coming-Out Day. Most frequently, people from across the region gather at a local private facility and share a potluck dinner. A guest speaker accompanies the dinner and leads the group in remembering where we have come from and where we need to go. We have also celebrated publicly with an open-mike night at a local coffee house. Similarly, the town meeting asks community members to take a critical look at our organization and redirect our mission and goals, ensuring that we serve the needs of the community.

Effecting Social Change

Over the last four years, we have witnessed significant changes in our local sociopolitical environment. For example, for our first festival, public park officers originally denied our request to use a public park. In our third year the same office welcomed our request and reserved the grounds without payment. Similarly, for our first festival, police authorities ignored our requests for protection. Now they too welcome our requests and our dollars. During our first year several lawyers turned us down when we requested legal representation to obtain nonprofit status. Now lawyers advertise in our programs and newsletters.

The day before the first festival, in response to several newspaper stories covering the anticipated festival, newspapers and television stations received numerous phone calls threatening to boycott and vandalize their businesses if they covered the event. In subsequent years, we have documented no such calls. Similarly, during the first festival, protestors held a rally against the festival the night before outside the county court office, and people picketed along the perimeter of the festival. Since then, we have observed fewer demonstrations, and last year there were none.

Furthermore, after the first festival, there was an uproar in the town about the use of city resources by a group of people who engage in immoral and illegal activities. This debate took place over several months in the city's newspaper and became an issue in the televised city council meetings. The city council members and the mayor publicly affirmed our right to assemble. Though local media still cover our festivals, since the first year we have noticed a steady decline in the negative editorials in the local newspaper, and an increase in the number of editorials in support of our work and of civil rights for all people.

Two years ago, we pressured the city council to include sexuality in the antidiscrimination clause protecting city employees. We still hope to pass the amendment. We also hope to join local business organizations and to cultivate more economically and politically powerful heterosexual allies, including business owners, church leaders, and politicians.

Our work has also received national and state attention. After our first year we received the "Most Organized Gay Pride Group" award in our state. The NGLTF sent a member of their board of directors to our 1996 festival to speak. Also, in 1996, a national church chose our town for its first ordination of over twenty gay priests from around the country. The ordination coincided with our festival. We now are solicited by national musical and acting groups to play at our events, and national celebrities have donated items for an auction to benefit our organizations. Furthermore, over the last two years we have received three small grants from philanthropic organizations located outside our state. These grants support activities that protect or establish civil rights in southern communities.

CONCLUSION

I began this project wanting to bridge the division between gay men and straight men, a division that feeds gender inequality among men and between men and women. I wanted to learn how to motivate straight men to not subordinate and devalue gay men and how to motivate gay men to not accept the demeaning labels and social status that straight men assign them. While answering these questions I helped create social change. It is this integration of research and activism that defines, for me, participatory research. I have learned in doing this research that good sociology and good activism can coexist.

I believe this study contributes to the questions I set out to answer. In particular I think my findings supporting Bem's (1995) idea of embracing rather than rejecting gender shows great promise in motivating men, though it does have limitations. Further, my findings regarding the influence of taking the role of other in men's lives may prove to be a very important element in the social construction of egalitarian identities. I am proud of my activism and look forward to continuing it. There is a long way to go.

Appendix A

Interview Guide for Gay Men

Introduction

1. Tell me about yourself—where you grew up, age, education, job, family (probe: past and present).

Friendships

1. Tell me about your friendship with _____? How long have you been friends? How did you meet? What do you like to do together?
2. What do you *like* about ____? Can you remember complimenting ____ about any of these things you like? When was it? If so, what happened? If not, why not? Can you remember receiving a compliment from ____? What happened in that conversation?
3. What was one of the *best times* you had with ____ (probe: times when they did something they both enjoyed, a special conversation, times when one of them helped the other out)? Where were you? What were you doing?
4. Do you ever talk with ____ about things going on in your life (probe: family, work, school, relationships, decisions, problems, accomplishments. . . . probe for intimacy)? If not, why not? If so, what have you talked about with him recently? How did ____ react? Is there anything you won't discuss with ____? Why not? Does ____ talk with you about what is going on in his life? If not, why not? If so, what has he recently talked with you about? How did you react? Do you think you were helpful? Is there anything ____ doesn't discuss with you? Why not?

5. If it doesn't come up in above conversation: (a) Have you ever felt happy, compassion, sad, worried for ____? Did you express this to him? If so, what happened? If not, why not? (b) Have you ever cried or been upset in front of ____? How did he react? Has ____ ever cried or been upset in front of you? How did you react? (c) Do you love him? Have you ever hugged him? (d) Do you trust ____? Do you have any secrets you shared with him?

6. What do you *dislike* about ____? Have you ever told ____ about any of these things you dislike? When was it? If so, what happened in that conversation? If not, why not? Has ____ ever told you about something you do that bothers him? When was it? What happened in that conversation?

7. What was one of the *worst times* you had with ____ (probe: problems, conflict, argument)? Can you describe an occasion with ____ when you felt (a) anger, (b) shame, (c) embarrassment, (d) anxiety, (e) resentment . . . ? Did you express this to him? If so, what happened? If not, why not? Has ____ ever expressed (a) anger, (b) frustration, (c) guilt, (d) embarrassment with you? If so, what happened?

Coming Out

1. Tell me about when you came out to ____. Where were you? What were you doing together at the time? How did you tell him? How did he react?

2. When did you first think about coming out to him? What were the issues you considered? Did you talk to anyone about doing it? If so, what did you talk about? What did they say?

3. How did you feel? Did you talk to anyone about them? If so, what did you tell them? What did they say? (Probe: How did you deal with those feelings?)

4. Has ____ ever been with you and your partner/or a date? If not, why not? If so, did you act any differently because ____ was there? Did you express affection for your partner/date in front of ____ (probe: hand holding, arm around him, a kiss)? If not, why not? If so, how did ____ react?

Other Friendships

1. Do you have any other close friendships with other gay or straight men? What kinds of things do you do with them? What kinds of things do you talk about with them?
2. Do you ever do things with several of your friends together (probe: going to parties, going out)? If so, what happened? If not, why not? If you were to have a party at your house would you invite your straight friends and gay friends?

Appendix B

Interview Guide for Straight Men

Introduction

1. Tell me about yourself—where you grew up, age, education, job, family (probe: past and present).

Friendships

1. Tell me about your friendship with _____? How long have you been friends? How did you meet? What do you like to do together?
2. What do you *like* about _____? Can you remember complimenting _____ about any of these things you like? When was it? If so, what happened? If not, why not? Can you remember receiving a compliment from _____? What happened in that conversation?
3. What was one of the *best times* you had with _____ (probe: times when they did something they both enjoyed, a special conversation, times when one of them helped the other out)? Where were you? What were you doing?
4. Do you ever talk with _____ about things going on in your life (probe: family, work, school, relationships, decisions, problems, accomplishments. . . . probe for intimacy)? If not, why not? If so, what have you talked about with him recently? How did _____ react? Is there anything you won't discuss with _____? Why not? Does _____ talk with you about what is going on in his life? If not, why not? If so, what has he recently talked with you about? How did you react? Do you think you were helpful? Is there anything _____ doesn't discuss with you? Why not?

5. If it doesn't come up in above conversation: (a) Have you ever felt happy, compassion, sad, worried for ____? Did you express this to him? If so, what happened? If not, why not? (b) Have you ever cried or been upset in front of ____? How did he react? Has ____ ever cried or been upset in front of you? How did you react? (c) Do you love him? Have you ever hugged him? (d) Do you trust ____? Do you have any secrets you shared with him?

6. What do you *dislike* about ____? Have you ever told ____ about any of these things you dislike? When was it? If so, what happened in that conversation? If not, why not? Has ____ ever told you about something you do that bothers him? When was it? What happened in that conversation?

7. What was one of the *worst times* you had with ____ (probe: problems, conflict, argument)? Can you describe an occasion with ____ when you felt (a) anger, (b) shame, (c) embarrassment, (d) anxiety, (e) resentment . . . ? Did you express this to him? If so, what happened? If not, why not? Has ____ ever expressed (a) anger, (b) frustration, (c) guilt, (d) embarrassment with you? If so, what happened?

Coming Out

1. Tell me about what happened when ____ came out to you? Where were you? What were you doing together at the time? How did he tell you? How did you react? How did he react to you?

2. When ____ came out to you how did you feel? Did you talk to any one about how you felt? If so, who and how? What did they say? (Probe: how did you deal with those feelings?)

3. Have you ever been with ____ and his partner/or date? How did you react? If not, would you want to spend time with ____ and his partner/date? Have you ever seen ____ express affection for another man (probe: hand holding, arm around him, a kiss)? How did you react? If you haven't seen this, how do you think you would react if you did?

Other Friendships

1. Did you tell any of your other straight friends that you have a gay friend? (a) If so, how? Why? How did they react? (b) If not, why not? How do you think they would react? How do you think they would react toward you?
2. Have any of your other friends' actual or anticipated reactions to you having a gay friend changed your relationship with them? How so? Have any of your other friends actual or anticipated reactions changed your relationship with ____? How so?
3. Do you ever do things with several of your friends together (probe: going to parties, going out)? If so, when was it? What did you all do together? How did it go? If not, why not? If you were to have a party at your house would you invite your straight friends and gay friends?

Appendix C

Informed Consent

Ms. Price has informed me of the nature and purpose of her study on friendships between gay and straight men; informed me of the terms of my participation in the study; and assured me confidentiality. I understand that I do not have to answer any questions I do not wish to answer, and that I can end the interview at any time. I voluntarily agree to participate in this study.

_____

Participant Name—Printed

_____

Participant Signature

_____

Jammie Price

Appendix D

Transcription Confidentiality

I have been hired by Ms. Price to transcribe some of her taped interviews. She has informed me of the nature and purpose of her study on friendships between gay and straight men. I have assured Ms. Price that I will maintain the anonymity, where possible, and confidentiality she promised her study participants. I will not share any of the information I hear while transcribing or discuss her study with other people.

_____

Typist Name—Printed

_____

Typist Signature

_____

Jammie Price

Notes

Introduction

1. The increase in gay-hate crimes could be due to higher reporting rates. Surveys of gay populations indicate the increase is due to rising amounts of victimization (Herek, 1989).

Chapter 1

1. Cross-sexual friendships are less rare among women (Nardi and Sherrod, 1990, 1994; Nardi, 1992b).

2. See also the work of Shields (1987) and Hochschild (1983) on how people use emotions to signify their own and evaluate other's gender identity.

3. Scheff (1988, 1990a,b) refers to the process by which we anticipate, experience, or avoid shame in order to feel pride the "deference-emotion system."

4. People can target different emotion processes to "work" on: (1) with cognitive strategies people attempt to change images, ideas, or thoughts associated with feelings; (2) with bodily strategies people attempt to change physical symptoms of emotions such as crying, shaking, and perspiring; and (3) with expressive strategies, people attempt to change expressive gestures to change feeling such as smiling (Hochschild, 1979:562).

5. Masculinity and femininity are not mutually exclusive; men and women can identify with and practice both femininity and masculinity (Brittan, 1989). Multiple masculinities and femininities exist, varying across class, race, ethnicity, sexuality, life course, cohort, time, and place (Connell, 1995; Segal, 1990; Kimmel, 1992).

6. While many gay men construct masculinity in this fashion, many do not. Studies of gay men show that some gay and heterosexual men practice masculinity similarly (Connell, Davis, and Dowsett, 1993; Connell, 1992). Many gay men are not effeminate. Further, many homosexual men see themselves as more similar to heterosexual than homosexual men (Simon, Glassner-Bayerl, and Stratenwerth, 1991). Overall, as much diversity exists in how gay men practice masculinities and femininities as in how heterosexual men do (Risman and Schwartz, 1988; Callender and Kochems, 1985).

7. In contrast, heterosexual men tend to see lesbians as sexual deviants rather than as gender deviants (Price and Dalecki, 1998). They acknowledge more variation among lesbians, who may be effeminate or masculine or neither, and who may or may not have personalities and behaviors similar to heterosexual women.

Given the wide range of gender options that women experience, this is not surprising. Women, straight and lesbian, can be effeminate or masculine, or neither or both, and still be within the range of socially appropriate behavior. The only thing that lesbians consistently do differently from straight women is to have sex with women rather than men.

Chapter 2

1. The term "queer" includes gay men, lesbians, bisexuals, and transgenderists. Queer people generally prefer this term over the term "gay" when referring to nonheterosexual persons (Irvine, 1994). However, people still frequently use the terms "gay community," "gay pride," and "gay rights," so I follow suit. The terms "transgenderist" and "transsexual" are also often used interchangeably. I tend to use the term "transgenderist" because it is more inclusive.

2. The bar manager was not concerned about me soliciting customers. He was concerned about losing money. So he granted me permission to do research regularly on weekday nights but not on weekend nights because that is when the bar makes the most money. During the week I did not have to pay cover charges. I went on several Friday and Saturday nights over the course of the study period, paying full price.

Chapter 3

1. Through interaction in the gay community, queer people learn vocabulary, mannerisms, and ways of joking (Goodwin, 1989; Sprague, 1984). In turn, appropriate use of the language, mannerisms, and ways of joking signifies membership in the gay community (Moon, 1995; Herdt, 1992). It denotes that you can be trusted, that you mean no harm. This aspect of gay culture parallels how African Americans can joke, tease, and talk about race, but white Americans cannot (Franklin, 1992; Abrahams, 1976; Brown, 1972), at least not without being suspected of racism. It is a discourse that belongs to members of the African-American community, to which white Americans are assumed not to belong. When African Americans joke about race it signifies their community membership. African Americans see white Americans making racial jokes as a form of blasphemy of their culture, community, and trust.

2. Research shows that in most friendships and romantic relationships between men and women, women do most of the emotion work (Hochschild, 1983, 1989; Shields, 1987).

3. The term "reading" in the gay community refers to observing someone's behavior and appearance to determine if they are queer. "Clocking" is a synonym.

4. See Myers (1996) for a similar discussion on how white women are incensed by the same racist remarks that black women find mundane.

5. I asked the gay men why they thought the straight man in these examples was gay. All of them chalked it up to "gaydar." Gaydar is their acquired ability to

detect other queer people. They acquire this skill from being around queer people. The signals can be subtle: the way a man talks, makes eye contact, moves or holds his body, or his choice of clothing.

Chapter 4

1. All the gay men in my study hold essentialist beliefs about the origin of their sexuality. They believe they were born homosexual. For some men, though, it took many years to realize or accept it. When they do, they "come out to themselves."

2. I discuss the gay man's gender and sexual identity in Chapter 6.

3. Internalized homophobia is most intense among young queer people and queer people who are not out. It likely continues to some degree as queer people age or come out because they continue to face hostile attitudes, values, beliefs, and social contexts (Meyer, 1995; Troiden, 1989).

Chapter 5

1. I interviewed the men in these friendships because they defined the friendship as "close." After the interview with them I realized that they were not close, according to standard definitions in the friendship literature (Hays, 1989).

2. By intentionally making people aware of their discomfort with homosexuality you call attention to and establish a recognizable gay identity, culture, and community (Chauncey, 1994; Seidman, 1993; D'Emilio, 1983).

Chapter 6

1. For a similar discussion on how racism bonds African Americans see Mays, Cochran, and Rhue (1994).

Chapter 7

1. From what I saw and know about the gay community from my field work, my sample represents the remaining gender variation among the gay men in this community. Some of the gay men I interviewed are drag queens, some are gender neutral, and some appear straight.

2. For example, the macho gay men I saw wear clothes associated with very masculine men such as leather jackets and black leather boots, or denim jackets and construction boots, or military uniforms. Many wear beards and mustaches. They ride motorcycles or drive trucks. They act tough and emotionally reserved.

3. In an article titled "Insult and Inclusion: The Term *Fag Hag* and Gay Male Community," Moon (1995) discusses at length the sexism inherent in this term, who uses it, and what it means to members of the gay community.

4. For example, one "straight" man called me to set up an interview. Shortly into the interview he revealed that his gay friend was a homeless man whom he met in a city he was visiting for a day. He then confessed that he was in the process of coming out and that this interview was a step in that process. I was the first straight person he had told. I did not include this interview in my analysis.

5. The gay man with AIDS did seek help for his depression and is still in therapy today. Through my activist work I see and talk with him about once a month. I do not know whether the incest victim or either of the straight men ever sought counseling. I never saw the two straight men again. I have seen the incest victim several times but always in the company of others, where it would not have been appropriate to raise this question.

References

Abrahams, R.D. 1976. *Talking Back*. Rowley, MA: Newbury House.

Acker, Joan. 1990. "Hierarchies, jobs, bodies: A theory of gendered organizations." *Gender and Society* 4(2):139-158.

Albas, Cheryl and Daniel Albas. 1988. "Emotion work and emotion rules: The case of exams." *Qualitative Sociology* 11(4):259-274.

Allan, G. 1989. *Friendship: Developing a Sociological Perspective*. Boulder, CO: Westview.

American Medical Association, Council on Scientific Affairs. 1996. "Health care needs of gay men and lesbians in the US." *Journal of the American Medical Association* 275(17):1354-1359.

Anderson, Margaret and Patricia Hill Collins. 1994. *Race, Class, and Gender: An Anthology*, Second Edition. Belmont, CA: Wadsworth.

Aries, E. 1976. "Interaction patterns and themes in male, female, and mixed-sex groups." *Small Group Behavior* 7:7-18.

Bell, Allen P. and Martin Weinberg. 1978. *Homosexualities: A Study of Diversity Among Men and Women*. New York: Simon and Schuster.

Bell, R. 1981. *Worlds of Friendship*. Beverly Hills, CA: Sage.

Bell, S.E. 1988. "Becoming a political woman: The reconstruction and interpretation of experience through stories," in A.D. Todd and S. Fisher (Eds.) *Gender and Discourse: The Power of Talk*. Norwood, NJ: Ablex.

Bem, Sandra Lipsitz. 1976. "Probing the promise of androgyny," pp. 48-62 in A.G. Kaplan and J.P. Bean (Eds.) *Beyond Sex-Role Stereotypes: Readings Toward a Psychology of Androgyny*. Boston: Little, Brown.

———— 1995. "Dismantling gender polarization and compulsory heterosexuality: Should we turn the volume down or up?" *The Journal of Sex Research* 32(4):329-334.

Berger, R.M. and Mallon, D. 1993. "Social support networks of gay men." *Journal of Sociology and Social Welfare* 20(1):155-174.

Billy, J.O.G., K. Tanfer, W.R. Grady, and D.H. Klepinger. 1993. "The sexual behavior of men in the United States." *Family Planning Perspectives* 25:52-60.

Binson, D., S. Michaels, R. Stall, T.J. Coates, J.H. Gagnon, and J.A. Catania. 1995. "Prevalence and social distribution of men who have sex with men: United States and its urban centers." *Journal of Sex Research* 32:245-254.

Bird, Sharon R. 1996. "Welcome to the men's club: Homosociality and the maintenance of hegemonic masculinity." *Gender and Society* 10(2):120-132.

Black, Kathryn N. and Michael R. Stevenson. 1984. "The relationship of self-reported sex-role characteristics and attitudes toward homosexuality." *Journal of Homosexuality* 10(1/2):83-93.

Blieszner, Rosemary and Rebecca G. Adams. 1992. *Adult Friendship*. Newbury Park, CA: Sage.

Blumer, Herbert. 1969. *Symbolic Interactionism: Perspective and Method*. Berkeley, CA: University of California.

Bornstein, K. 1994. *Gender Outlaw: On Men, Women, and the Rest of Us*. New York: Random House.

Brittan, Arthur. 1989. *Masculinity and Power*. New York: Basil Blackwell.

Brod, Harry. 1987. "Introduction: Themes and theses of men's studies," pp. 1-20 in H. Brod (Ed.) *The Making of Masculinities: The New Men's Studies*. Boston: Allen and Unwin.

Brown, Claude. 1972. "The language of soul," pp. 134-39 in T. Kochman (Ed.) *Rappin' and Stylin' Out: Communication in Urban Black America*. Champaigne, IL: University of Illinois.

Buhrke, R.A. and D.R. Fuqua. 1987. "Sex differences in same- and cross-sex supportive relationships." *Sex Roles* 17:339-352.

Burt, Ronald. 1982. *Toward a Structural Theory of Action*. New York: Academic.

Callender, C. and L.M. Kochems. 1985. "Men and non-men: Male gender-mixing statuses and homosexuality." *Journal of Homosexuality* 11(3-4):165-178.

Carrigan, Tim, Bob Connell, and John Lee. 1985. "Toward a new sociology of masculinity." *Theory and Society* 14(5):551-604.

Chauncey, G. 1994. *Gay New York: Gender, Urban Culture, and the Making of the Gay Male World 1890-1940*. New York: Basic.

Clark, Candace. 1987. "Sympathy biography and sympathy margin." *American Journal of Sociology* 93(2):290-321.

———— 1990. "Emotions and micropolitics in everyday life: Some patterns and paradoxes of place," pp. 305-333 in T. Kemper (Ed.) *Research Agendas in the Sociology of Emotions*. New York: State University of New York.

Clatterbaugh, Kenneth. 1990. *Contemporary Perspectives on Masculinity: Men, Women and Politics in Modern Society*. Boulder, CO: Westview.

Cochran, S.D. and V.M. Mays. 1994. "Depressive distress among homosexually active African-American men and women. *American Journal of Psychiatry* 151:524-29.

Cockburn, Cynthia. 1983. *Brothers: Male Dominance and Technological Change*. London: Pluto.

———— 1991. *In the Way of Women: Men's Resistance to Sex Equality in Organizations*. Ithaca, NY: ILR.

Collins, Patricia Hill. 1990. *Black Feminist Thought: Knowledge, Consciousness, and the Politics of Empowerment*. New York: Routledge.

Collinson, D.L. 1988. "Engineering honour: Masculinity, joking and conflict in shop floor relations." *Organizational Studies* 9:181-189.

Comstock, G.D. 1991. *Violence Against Lesbians and Gay Men*. New York: Columbia University.

Connell, R.W. 1987. *Gender and Power*. Stanford, CA: Stanford University.
―――― 1990. "A whole new world: Remaking masculinity in the context of the environmental movement." *Gender and Society* 4:452-478.
―――― 1991. "Live fast and die young: The construction of masculinity among young working-class men on the margin of the labour market." *Australian and New Zealand Journal of Sociology* 27:141-171.
―――― 1992. "A very strange gay: Masculinity, homosexual experience, and the dynamics of gender." *American Sociological Review* 57:735-751.
―――― 1993. "The big picture: Masculinities in recent world history." *Theory and Society* 22(5):597-624.
―――― 1995. *Masculinities*. Berkeley, CA: University of California.
Connell, R.W., M.D. Davis, and G.W. Dowsett. 1993. "A bastard of a life: Homosexual desire and practice among men in working-class milieux." *Australian and New Zealand Journal of Sociology* 29(1):112-135.
Coxon, Tony, P.M. Davies, A.J. Hunt, T.J. McManus, C.M. Rees, and P. Weatherburn. 1993. "Research note: Strategies in eliciting sensitive sexual information: The case of gay men." *Sociological Review* 41(3):537-555.
Crawford, June, Susan Kippax, Jenny Onyx, Una Gault and Pam Benton. 1992. *Emotion and Gender: Constructing Meaning from Memory*. London: Sage.
Davidson, L.R. and L. Duberman. 1982. "Friendship: Communication and interactional patterns in same-sex dyads." *Sex Roles* 8:809-822.
D'Emilio, J. 1983. *Sexual Politics, Sexual Communities: The Making of a Homosexual Minority in the United States, 1940-1970*. Chicago: University of Chicago.
Doll, L.S., L.R. Petersen, C.R. White, E.S. Johnson, and J.W. Ward. 1992. "Homosexually and nonhomosexually identified men who have sex with men: A behavioral comparison." *Journal of Sex Research* 29:1-14.
Donaldson, Mike. 1993. "What is hegemonic masculinity." *Theory and Society* 22(5):643-658.
Dowsett, G.W. 1993. "I'll show you mine, if you'll show me yours: Gay men, masculinity research, men's studies, and sex." *Theory and Society* 22(5):697-709.
Duck, S., and P.H. Wright. 1993. "Re-examining gender differences in same-gender friendships: A close look at two kinds of data." *Sex Roles* 28:709-727.
Fay, R.E., C.F. Turner, A.D. Klassen, and J.H. Gagnon. 1989. "Prevalence and patterns of same-gender sexual contact among men." *Science* 243:338-348.
Ficarrotto, Thomas J. 1990. "Racism, sexism, and erotophobia: Attitudes of heterosexuals toward homosexuals." *Journal of Homosexuality* 19(1):111-116.
Fish, Thomas A. and Barbara J. Rye. 1991. "Attitudes toward a homosexual or heterosexual person with AIDS." *Journal of Applied Social Psychology* 21(8):651-667.
Flam, H. 1990. "Emotional 'man': Corporate actors as emotion-motivated emotion managers." *International Sociology* 5(1):39-56.
Franklin II, C. 1992. "Friendship among black men," pp. 201-214 in P.M. Nardi (Ed.) *Men's Friendship*. Newbury Park, CA: Sage.

Gaelick, L., G.V. Bodenhausen, and R.S. Wyer. 1985. "Emotional communication in close relationships." *Journal of Personality and Social Psychology* 49(5):1246-1265.

Gergen, M.M. 1988. "Narrative structures in social explanation." In C. Antaki (Ed.) *Analyzing Everyday Explanation: A Casebook of Methods.* Newbury Park, CA: Sage.

Goffman, E. 1963. *Stigma: Notes on the Management of a Spoiled Identity.* Englewood Cliffs, NJ: Prentice-Hall.

―――― 1967. *Interaction Ritual.* New York: Anchor.

―――― 1976. "Gender display." *Studies in the Anthropology of Visual Communication* 3:69-77.

Goodwin, J.P. 1989. *More Man Than You'll Ever Be: Gay Folklore and Acculturation in Middle America.* Bloomington, IN: Indiana University.

Gordon, Steven. 1990. "Social structural effects on emotions," pp. 145-179 in T. Kemper (Ed.) *Research Agendas in the Sociology of Emotions.* New York: State University of New York.

Halper, Jan. 1988. *Quiet Desperation: The Truth About Successful Men.* New York: Warner.

Hays, R.B. 1989. "The day-to-day functioning of close versus casual friendships." *Journal of Social and Personal Relationships* 6:21-37.

Hays, R.B., J.A. Catania, W. McKusick, and T.J. Coates. 1990. "Help-seeking for AIDS-related concerns: A comparison of gay men with various HIV diagnoses." *American Journal of Community Psychology* 18(5):743-755.

Herdt, G. 1992. *Gay Culture in America: Essays from the Field.* Boston: Beacon.

Herek, Gregory M. 1984a. "Attitudes toward lesbians and gay men: A factor-analytic study." *Journal of Homosexuality* 10(1/2):39-51.

―――― 1984b. "Beyond homophobia: A social psychological perspective on attitudes toward lesbians and gay men." *Journal of Homosexuality* 10(1/2):1-21.

―――― 1987. "On heterosexual masculinity: Some psychological consequences of the social construction of gender and sexuality," pp. 68-82 in M. Kimmel (Ed.) *Changing Men: New Directions in Research on Men and Masculinity.* Newbury Park, CA: Sage.

―――― 1989. "Hate crimes against lesbians and gay men: Issues for research and policy." *American Psychologist* 44(6):948-955.

Hochschild, Arlie R. 1979. "Emotion work, feeling rules and social structure." *American Journal of Sociology* 85(3):551-575.

―――― 1983. *The Managed Heart: Commercialization of Human Feeling.* Berkeley, CA: University of California.

―――― 1989. "The economy of gratitude," pp. 95-114 in D.D. Franks and E. Doyle McCarthy (Eds.) *The Sociology of Emotions: Original Essays and Research Papers.* Greenwich, CT: JAI.

―――― 1990. "Ideology and emotion management: A perspective and path for future research," pp. 117-142 in T. Kemper (Ed.) *Research Agendas in the Sociology of Emotions.* New York: State University of New York.

hooks, bell. 1984. *Feminist Theory: From Margin to Center.* Boston: South End.

House, J.S. 1977. "The three faces of social psychology." *Sociometry* 40:161-177.

Irvine, Janice M. 1994. "A place in the rainbow: Theorizing lesbian and gay culture." *Sociological Theory* 12(2):232-248.

Kane, Emily W. and Laura J. Macaulay. 1993. "Interviewer gender and gender attitudes." *Public Opinion Quarterly* 57:1-28.

Kemper, Theodore D. 1990. *Research Agendas in the Sociology of Emotions.* New York: State University of New York.

Kennedy, E.L. and M.D. Davis. 1993. *Boots of Leather, Slippers of Gold: The History of a Lesbian Community.* New York: Routledge.

Kimmel, Michael. 1992. "Reading men: Men, masculinity, and publishing." *Contemporary Sociology* 21(2):162-171.

King, K. 1990. "Producing sex, theory, and culture: Gay/straight remappings in contemporary feminism," pp. 82-101 in M. Hirsch and E.F. Keller (Eds.) *Conflicts in Feminism.* New York: Routledge.

Klassen, A.D., C.J. Williams, and E.E. Levitt. 1989. *Sex and Morality in the United States.* Middletown, CT: Wesleyan University.

Kohn, Melvin L. 1989. "Social structure and personality: A quintessentially sociological approach to social psychology." *Social Forces* 68:26-33.

Kurdek, L. and J.P. Schmitt. 1987. "Perceived emotional support from families and friends in members of homosexual, married and heterosexual cohabiting couples." *Journal of Homosexuality* 14:57-68.

Laumann, E.O., J.H. Gagnon, R.T. Michael, and S. Michaels. 1994. *The Social Organization of Sexuality: Sexual Practices in the United States.* Chicago: University of Chicago.

Lehne, Gregory K. 1989. "Homophobia among men: Supporting and defining the male role," pp. 416-429 in M. Kimmel and M. Messner (Eds.) *Men's Lives.* New York: Macmillan.

Lewis, Robert A. 1978. "Emotional intimacy among men." *Journal of Social Issues* 34(1):108-121.

Lorber, Judith and Susan Farrell. 1991. *Social Construction of Gender.* Newbury Park, CA: Sage.

MacKinnon, Catherine. 1989. *Toward a Feminist Theory of the State.* Cambridge, MA: Harvard University.

Majors, R. 1989. "Cool pose: The proud signature of black survival," pp. 83-87 in M. Kimmel and M. Messner (Eds.) *Men's Lives.* New York: Macmillan.

Martin, J.L. 1987. "The impact of AIDS on gay male sexual behavior patterns in New York City." *American Journal of Public Health* 77(5):578-581.

Mays, V.M., S.D. Cochran, and S. Rhue. 1994. "The impact of perceived discrimination on the intimate relationships of black lesbians." *Journal of Homosexuality* 25:1-14.

Mead, G.H. 1934. *Mind, Self and Society.* Chicago: University of Chicago.

Messner, Michael A. 1989. "Masculinities and athletic careers." *Gender and Society* 3:71-88.

———— 1992. *Power at Play: Sports and the Problem of Masculinity.* Boston: Beacon.

_____ 1993. "Changing men and feminist politics in the United States." *Theory and Society* 22(5):723-738.

Meyer, Ilan H. 1995. "Minority stress and mental health in gay men." *Journal of Health and Social Behavior* 36(March):38-56.

Miles, Matthew B. and A. Michael Huberman. 1994. *Qualitative Data Analysis.* Beverly Hills, CA: Sage.

Miller, S. 1983. *Men and Friendship.* Boston: Houghton Mifflin.

Mishler, E.G. 1984. *The Discourse of Medicine.* Norwood, NJ: Ablex.

Moon, D. 1995. "Insult and inclusion: The term *fag hag* and gay male 'community'." *Social Forces* 74(2):487-510.

Morgan, David. 1992. *Discovering Men.* London: Routledge.

Morgan, David and Michael Schwalbe. 1990. "Mind and self in society: Linking social structure and social cognition." *Social Psychology Quarterly* 53(2):148-164.

Myers, Kristen. 1996. *Sailing Under False Colors: Race, Class and Gender in a Women's Organization.* Sociology Dissertation. Raleigh, NC: North Carolina State University.

Namaste, Ki. 1994. "The politics of inside/out: Queer theory, poststructuralism, and a sociological approach to sexuality." *Sociological Theory* 12(2):220-231.

Nardi, Peter M. 1992a. *Men's Friendships.* Newbury Park, CA: Sage.

_____ 1992b. "That's what friends are for: Friends as family in the gay and lesbian community," pp. 108-120 in K. Plummer (Ed.) *Modern Homosexualities: Fragments of Lesbian and Gay Experience.* London: Routledge.

Nardi, P.M. and D. Sherrod. 1990. "Friendship survey: The results." *Out/Look* 2(4):86.

_____ 1994. "Friendships in the lives of gay men and lesbians." *Journal of Social and Personal Relationships* 11:185-199.

Odets, W. 1995. *In the Shadow of the Epidemic: Being HIV-Negative in the Age of AIDS.* Durham, NC: Duke University.

Ostrow, D.G. and P.A. Wren. 1992. *Comprehensive HIV/AIDS Mental Health Education Program (CHAM-HEP), I: Mental Health Aspects of HIV/AIDS.* Ann Arbor, MI: University of Michigan.

Peplau, L.A., S.D. Cochran, and V.M. Mays. 1997. "A national survey of the intimate relationships of African American lesbians and gay men," pp. 11-38 in B. Greene (Ed.) *Ethnic and Cultural Diversity Among Lesbians and Gay Men.* Newbury Park, CA: Sage.

Price, Jammie and Michael Dalecki. 1998. "The social basis of homophobia: An empirical illustration." *Sociological Spectrum* 18(2):143-159.

Rawlins, W.K. 1992. *Friendship Matters: Communication, Dialectics, and the Life Course.* New York: Aldine de Gruyter.

Reisman, J.M. 1990. "Intimacy in same-sex friendships." *Sex Roles* 23:65-82.

Reskin, Barbara. 1988. "Bringing the men back in: Sex differentiation and the devaluation of women's work." *Gender and Society* 2(1):58-81.

Rich, Adrienne. 1980. "Compulsory heterosexuality and lesbian existence." *SIGNS* 5(4):660.

Ridgeway, Cecilia L. 1992. *Gender, Interaction and Inequality.* New York: Springer-Verlag.

Risman, Barbara. 1992. "Toward a post-gender society: A structural interactionist framework for understanding gender." Presented at the American Sociological Association Meetings.

Risman, Barbara and Pepper Schwartz. 1988. "Sociological research on male and female homosexuality." *Annual Review of Sociology* 14:125-147.

Rodgers, B. 1972. *The Queen's Vernacular: A Gay Lexicon.* San Francisco: Straight Arrow.

Rommetveit, Ragnar. 1974. *On Message: A Framework for the Study of Language and Communication.* New York: Wiley.

Rubin, G. S. 1993 [1984]. "Thinking sex: Notes for a radical theory of the politics of sexuality," pp. 3-44 in H. Abelove, M. Barale, and D.M. Halperin (Eds.) *The Lesbian and Gay Studies Reader.* New York: Routledge.

Rubin, Lillian B. 1983. *Intimate Strangers: Men and Women Together.* New York: Harper and Row.

Sattel, Jack W. 1976. "The inexpressive male: Tragedy or sexual politics?" *Social Problems* 23(4): 469-477.

Scheff, Thomas J. 1988. "Shame and conformity: The deference-emotion system." *American Sociological Review* 53:395-406.

―――― 1990a. *Microsociology: Discourse, Emotion, and Social Structure.* Chicago: University of Chicago.

―――― 1990b. "Socialization of emotions: Pride and shame as causal agents," pp. 281-304 in T. Kemper (Ed.) *Research Agendas in the Sociology of Emotions.* Albany, NY: State University of New York.

Schwalbe, Michael L. 1992. "Male supremacy and the narrowing of the moral Self." *Berkeley Journal of Sociology* 31:29-54.

Schwalbe, Michael L. and Clifford L. Staples. 1991. "Gender differences in sources of self-esteem." *Social Psychology Quarterly* 54:158-168.

Sedgwick, E.K. 1990. *Epistemology of the Closet.* Berkeley, CA: University of California.

Segal, Lynne. 1990. *Slow Motion: Changing Masculinity, Changing Men.* New Brunswick, NJ: Rutgers University.

―――― 1993. "Changing men: Masculinities in context." *Theory and Society* 22(5):625-642.

Seidler, Victor J. 1989. *Rediscovering Masculinity: Reason, Language and Sexuality.* London: Routledge.

―――― 1991a. *Recreating Sexual Politics: Men, Feminism and Politics.* London: Routledge.

―――― 1991b. *The Achilles Heel Reader: Men, Sexual Politics and Socialism.* London: Routledge.

―――― 1992. "Rejection, vulnerability, and friendship," pp. 15-34 in P. Nardi (Ed.) *Men's Friendships.* Newbury Park, CA: Sage.

Seidman, Steven. 1993. "Identity and politics in a 'postmodern' gay culture: Some historical and conceptual notes," pp. 105-142 in M. Warner (Ed.) *Fear of a Queer Planet: Queer Politics and Social Theory.* Minneapolis, MN: University of Minnesota.

———— 1994. "Queer-ing sociology, sociologizing queer theory: An introduction." *Sociological Theory* 12(2):166-177.

Sell, Jane, W.I. Griffith, and Rick K. Wilson. 1993. "Are women more cooperative than men in social dilemmas?" *Social Psychology Quarterly* 56(3):211-222.

Sewall, William H., Jr. 1992. "A theory of structure: Duality, agency, and transformation." *American Journal of Sociology* 98(July):1-29.

Sherrod, Drury. 1987. "The bonds of men: Problems and possibilities in close male relationships," pp. 213-239 in H. Brod (Ed.) *The Making of Masculinities: The New Men's Studies.* Boston: Allen and Unwin.

Shibutani, Tamotsu. 1987. *Society and Personality: An Interactionist Approach to Social Psychology.* New Brunswick, NJ: Transaction Books.

Shields, Stephanie A. 1987. "Women, men, and the dilemma of emotion," pp. 229-250 in P. Shaver and C. Hendrick (Eds.) *Sex and Gender.* Newbury Park, CA: Sage.

Shilts, Randy. 1987. *And the Band Played On: Politics, People, and the AIDS Epidemic.* New York: St. Martin's.

Shott, Susan. 1979. "Emotion and social life: A symbolic interactionist analysis." *American Journal of Sociology* 84(6):1317-1333.

Sigelman, Carol K., Jennifer L. Howell, David P. Cornell, John D. Cutright, and Janine C. Dewey. 1991. "Courtesy stigma: The social implications of associating with a gay person." *The Journal of Social Psychology* 131(1):45-56.

Simon, Bernd, Brigitta Glassner-Bayerl, and Ina Stratenwerth. 1991. "Stereotyping and self-stereotyping in a natural intergroup context: The case of heterosexual and homosexual men." *Social Psychology Quarterly* 54(3):252-266.

Smith, Allen C. and Sherryl Kleinman. 1989. "Managing emotions in medical school: Student's contacts with the living and the dead." *Social Psychology Quarterly* 52(1):56-69.

Smith, T.W. 1991. "Adult sexual behavior in 1989: Number of partners, frequency of intercourse and risk of AIDS." *Family Planning Perspectives* 23:102-107.

Snell, W. 1989. "Willingness to self-disclose to female and male friends as a function of social anxiety and gender." *Personality and Social Psychology Bulletin* 45:1061-1072.

Sprague, Gregory A. 1984. "Male homosexuality in Western culture: The dilemma of identity and subculture in historical research." *Journal of Homosexuality* 10(3/4):29-43.

Stanley, J.P. and S.J. Wolfe. 1980. *The Coming Out Stories.* Watertown, MA: Persephone.

Stoltenberg, John. 1989. *Refusing to Be a Man: Essays on Sex and Justice.* New York: Penguin.

Swain, Scott. 1989. "Covert intimacy: Closeness in men's friendships," pp. 71-86 in B. J. Risman and P. Schwartz (Eds.) *Gender in Intimate Relationships: A Microstructural Approach.* Belmont, CA: Wadsworth.

Tanfer, K. 1993. "National survey of men: Design and execution." *Family Planning Perspectives* 25:83-86.

Tannen, Deborah. 1990. *You Just Don't Understand: Women and Men in Conversation*. New York: Ballantine.

Troiden, R. 1988. *Gay and Lesbian Identity*. Dix Hills, NY: General Hall.

—— 1989. "The formation of homosexual identities." *Journal of Homosexuality* 17:43-73.

Walby, Sylvia. 1990. *Theorizing Patriarchy*. Oxford: Basil Blackwell.

Walker, Karen. 1994. "Men, women, and friendship: What they say, what they do." *Gender and Society* 8(2):246-265.

Walters, K. 1994. "I'm not friends the way she's friends: Ideological and behavioral constructions of masculinity in men's friendships." *Masculinities* 2(2):38-55.

Warner, M. 1993. *Fear of a Queer Planet: Queer Politics and Social Theory*. Minneapolis, MN: University of Minnesota.

Warren, Carol A.B. 1988. *Gender Issues in Field Research*. Newbury Park, CA: Sage.

Watters, J.K. and P. Biernacki. 1989. "Targeted sampling: Options for the study of hidden populations." *Social Problems* 36:416-430.

Weinberg, T.S. 1978. "On doing and being gay." *Journal of Homosexuality* 4(2):143-156.

Weiss, Robert. 1990. *Staying the Course: The Emotional and Social Lives of Men Who Do Well at Work*. New York: Free Press.

West, Candace and Don H. Zimmerman. 1987. "Doing gender." *Gender and Society* 1(2):125-151.

Weston, K. 1991. *Families We Choose: Lesbian, Gays, Kinship*. New York: Columbia University.

Williams, Christine L. and E. Joel Heikes. 1993. "The importance of researcher's gender in the in-depth interview: Evidence from two case studies of male nurses." *Gender and Society* 7(2):280-291.

Williams, Dorie Giles. 1985. "Gender, masculinity-femininity, and emotional intimacy in same-sex friendship." *Sex Roles* 12(5/6):587-600.

Yin, R.K. 1984. *Case Study Research: Design and Methods*. Newbury Park, CA: Sage.

Zurcher, Louis A. 1982. "The staging of emotion: A dramaturgical analysis." *Symbolic Interaction* 5(1):1-22.

—— 1985. "The war game: Organizational scripting and the expression of emotion." *Symbolic Interaction* 8(2):191-206.

Index

Page numbers followed by the letter "t" indicate tables.